The Inchon Invasion

Books in the Battles Series:

> Battles of The Twentieth Century <

The Inchon Invasion

by Earle Rice Jr.

Lucent Books, P.O. Box 289011, San Diego, CA 92198-9011

Library of Congress Cataloging-in-Publication Data

Rice, Earle.
     The Inchon invasion / by Earle Rice.
        p.   cm. — (Battles of the twentieth century)
     Includes bibliographical references and index.
     ISBN 1-56006-418-8 (lib. ed. : alk. paper)
     1. Korean War, 1950-1953—Campaigns—Korea (South)—Inchon—
Juvenile literature. [1. Korean War, 1950-1953.] I. Title. II. Series.
     DS918.2.I5R53   1996
     951.904'2—dc20   95-11698
                                                              CIP
                                                              AC

Contents

Foreword

Almost everyone would agree with William Tecumseh Sherman that war "is all hell." Yet the history of war, and battles in particular, is so fraught with the full spectrum of human emotion and action that it becomes a microcosm of the human experience. Soldiers' lives are condensed and crystallized in a single battle. As Francis Miller explains in his *Photographic History of the Civil War* when describing the war wounded, "It is sudden, the transition from marching bravely at morning on two sound legs, grasping your rifle in two sturdy arms, to lying at nightfall under a tree with a member forever gone."

Decisions made on the battlefield can mean the lives of thousands. A general's pique or indigestion can result in the difference between life and death. Some historians speculate, for example, that Napoleon's fateful defeat at Waterloo was due to the beginnings of stomach cancer. His stomach pain may have been the reason that the normally decisive general was sluggish and reluctant to move his troops. And what kept George McClellan from winning battles during the Civil War? Some scholars and contemporaries believe that it was simple cowardice and fear. Others argue that he felt a gut-wrenching unwillingness to engage in the war of attrition that was characteristic of that particular conflict.

Battle decisions can be magnificently brilliant and horribly costly. At the Battle of Thaspus in 47 B.C., for example, Julius Caesar, facing a numerically superior army, shrewdly ordered his troops onto a narrow strip of land bordering the sea. Just as he expected, his enemy thought he had accidentally trapped himself and divided their forces to surround his troops. By dividing their army, his enemy had given Caesar the strategic edge he needed to defeat them. Other battle orders result in disaster, as in the case of the Battle at Balaklava during the Crimean War in 1854. A British general gave the order to attack a force of withdrawing enemy Russians. But confusion in relaying the order resulted in the 670 men of the Light Brigade's charging in the wrong direction into certain death by heavy enemy cannon fire. Battles are the stuff of history on the grandest scale—their outcomes often determine whether nations are enslaved or liberated.

Moments in battles illustrate the best and worst of human character. In the feeling of terror and the us-versus-them attitude that accompanies war, the enemy can be dehumanized and treated with a contempt that is considered repellent in times of peace. At Wounded Knee, the distrust and anticipation of violence that grew between the Native Americans and American soldiers led to the senseless killing of ninety men, women, and children. And who can forget My Lai, where the deaths of old men, women, and children at the hands of American soldiers shocked an America already disillusioned with the Vietnam War. The murder of six million Jews will remain burned into the human conscience forever as the measure of man's inhumanity to man. These horrors cannot be forgotten. And yet, under the terrible conditions of battle, one can find acts of bravery, kindness, and altruism. During the Battle of Midway, the members of Torpedo Squadron 8, flying in hopelessly antiquated planes and without the benefit of air protection from fighters, tried bravely to fulfill their mission—to destroy the *Kido Butai,* the Japanese Carrier Striking Force. Without air support, the squadron was immediately set upon by Japanese fighters. Nevertheless, each bomber tried valiantly to hit his target. Each failed. Every man but one died in the effort. But by keeping the Japanese fighters busy, the squadron bought time and delayed further Japanese fighter attacks. In the aftermath of the Battle of Isandhlwana in South Africa in 1879, a force of thousands of Zulu warriors trapped a contingent of British troops in a small trading post. After repeated bloody attacks in which many died on both sides, the Zulus, their final victory certain, granted the remaining British their lives as a gesture of respect for their bravery. During World War I, American troops were so touched by the fate of French war orphans that they took up a collection to help them. During the Civil War, soldiers of the North and South would briefly forget that they were enemies and share smokes and coffee across battle lines during the endless nights. These acts seem all the more dramatic, more uplifting, because they indicate that people can continue to behave with humanity when faced with inhumanity.

Lucent Books' Battles Series highlights the vast range of the human character revealed in the ordeal of war. Dramatic narrative describes in exciting and accurate detail the commanders, soldiers, weapons, strategies, and maneuvers involved in each battle. Each volume includes a comprehensive historical context, explaining what brought the parties to war, the events leading to the battle, what factors made the battle important, and the effects it had on the larger war and later events.

The Battles Series also includes a chronology of important dates that gives students an overview, at a glance, of each battle. Sidebars create a broader context by adding enlightening details on leaders, institutions, customs, warships, weapons, and armor mentioned in the narration. Every volume contains numerous maps that allow readers to better visualize troop movements and strategies. In addition, numerous primary and secondary source quotations drawn from both past historical witnesses and modern historians are included. These quotations demonstrate to readers how and where historians derive information about past events. Finally, the volumes in the Battles Series provide a launching point for further reading and research. Each book contains a bibliography designed for student research, as well as a second bibliography that includes the works the author consulted while compiling the book.

Above all, the Battles Series helps illustrate the words of Herodotus, the fifth-century B.C. Greek historian now known as the "father of history." In the opening lines of his great chronicle of the Greek and Persian Wars, the world's first battle book, he set for himself this goal: "To preserve the memory of the past by putting on record the astonishing achievements both of our own and of other peoples; and more particularly, to show how they came into conflict."

Chronology of Events

2333 B.C.
Korea founded by Tan'gun.

A.D. 1259
Mongols under Kublai Khan conquer Korea.

1356
Korean general Yi Song-gye seizes control of Korean government.

1392
General Yi assumes Korean crown and establishes Yi dynasty.

1592
Japan intrudes in Korean affairs (and again in 1596).

1647
Manchus overrun Korea.

1866
American trading vessel *General Sherman* is attacked by Koreans in the Taedong River below Pyongyang.

1871
U.S. Marines land in Korea.

1882
Korea signs trade agreement with the United States.

1894
Japan sends troops to Korea to "protect Japanese interests."

1896–1904
Russia obtains mineral and timber rights in Korea.

1910
Japan annexes Korea after defeating Russia in the Russo-Japanese War of 1904–1905.

1919
Koreans stage unsuccessful revolt against the Japanese and establish a temporary government in Shanghai; Syngman Rhee is named president.

1931
Japan invades Manchuria from Korea and forms puppet state of Manchukuo.

1937
Japanese troops cross into China from Manchukuo; Sino-Japanese War commences.

1941
December 7 Japan attacks Pearl Harbor; the United States enters World War II.

1945
August 8 Soviet Union declares war on Japan.
September 2 Japan surrenders to Allied forces to end World War II; the Soviet Union and the United States occupy Korea, north and south of the 38th parallel, respectively.

1947
September Joint Chiefs of Staff declare Korea of little strategic value to the United States.

1948
May Syngman Rhee is elected president of the new Republic of South Korea.

August 15 U.S. occupation of Korea ends.

September 9 Democratic People's Republic of Korea is formed, with Soviet sponsored Kim Il-sung as North Korea's new leader.

1950
January Secretary of State Dean Acheson defines U.S. defense line in the Far East, excluding any mention of Korea.

June 25 North Korea People's Army (NKPA) crosses the 38th parallel and invades South Korea.

June 27 President Truman authorizes U.S. air and naval forces to support ROK forces.

June 28 Seoul falls to NKPA.

June 30 President Truman commits U.S. ground troops to combat in Korea.

July 1 Elements of U.S. 24th Infantry Division arrive in Korea.

July 3 Inchon falls; Major General William F. Dean establishes 24th Infantry Division command post in Taejon.

July 5 Task Force Smith engages NKPA at Osan in first U.S. ground action of the war.

July 6 First Battalion of the 24th Infantry Division's 34th Regiment fights delaying action against NKPA at Pyongtaek and Chonan.

July 10–18 U.S. 25th Infantry Division arrives in Korea.

July 13 Lieutenant General Walton H. Walker establishes headquarters at Taegu for the Eighth U.S. Army (EUSA).

July 18 Lead elements of the U.S. First Cavalry Division lands unopposed at Pohang on Korea's east coast.

July 20 Taejon falls; General Dean missing in action.

July 27 General of the Army Douglas MacArthur flies to Taegu to confer with General Walker; Walker delivers "stand-or-die" order.

August 2 First Provisional Marine Brigade arrives in Korea.

August 4 Naktong (Pusan) Perimeter established.

August 6–18 First Battle of Naktong Bulge.

August 7 Task Force Kean launches first American counterattack of the war near Chinju.

August 10–20 ROKs battle for Pohang on the east coast.

August 15–22 Battle of Bowling Alley.

August 25 General Dean is captured by NKPA soldiers.

August 31–September 19 Second Battle of Naktong Bulge.

September 7 The First Provisional Marine Brigade is withdrawn from action in the Naktong Bulge.

September 13 The First Provisional Marine Brigade is disbanded and made part of First Marine Division; marines embark at Pusan for Inchon invasion.

September 15 D-Day for Inchon invasion; Joint Task Force Seven begins Operation CHROMITE; the First Marine Division establishes beachhead ashore.

September 16 The First Marine Division advances three miles inland.

September 16–22 The Eighth Army breaks out of Pusan Perimeter.

September 17 The First Marine Division captures Kimpo airfield; the Seventh Marine Regiment lands at Inchon and rejoins First Marine Division.

September 18 The 32nd Infantry Regiment of the Seventh Infantry Division debarks at Inchon, the rest of the division to follow.

September 21 The Seventh Infantry Division seizes high ground near Anyang; the First Marine Division captures Yongdungpo and crosses the Han River; Major General Edward M. Almond of X Corps takes charge of Operation CHROMITE.

September 22 The Seventh Infantry Division captures airfield at Suwon; Battle of Seoul begins.

September 23–24 The First Marine Division battles for Smith's Ridge and breaks through NKPA defenses outside Seoul.

September 25 The First Marine Division attacks Seoul from the west and south; the Seventh Infantry Division and the 17th ROK Regiment strike the city from the east.

September 26 General MacArthur releases United Nations Communiqué 9 announcing the liberation of Seoul one day too soon.

September 27 Eighth Army links up with X Corps near Osan. Seoul is liberated by the First Marine Division, the Seventh Infantry Division, and ROK Army and Marine Corps units.

September 29 General MacArthur officially returns Seoul to ROK president Syngman Rhee.

October 7 Operation CHROMITE ends.

INTRODUCTION

The North and the South

Korea ranks among the world's oldest countries. Its roots extend deep into centuries past. Korea's oral history speaks of its founding by Tan'gun in 2333 B.C. Tan'gun is said to have been the child of a divine creator and a maiden transformed from a bear. Korea's recorded history did not begin until twenty-one centuries after his passing. Warriors of the Chinese Han dynasty moved into northern Korea during the second century B.C. They established colonies and introduced Koreans to the written word. The Chinese also introduced a pattern of invasion, occupation, and repression.

Held captive by its own geography, Korea has struggled for centuries to resist the aggressions of its neighbors. China lies to the east, Japan to the west, and the Mongol nations (and more recently Russia) to the north. Each in its time has interfered with Korea's attempts to preserve its own heritage and culture.

The Hermit Kingdom

Koreans endured a long succession of Chinese and Mongol rules until the twentieth century. The Mongols under Kublai Khan first conquered the Chinese Northern Sung dynasty and then conquered Korea as well in A.D. 1259. But the Mongol rule lasted less than a century. In 1356 the Chinese Ming dynasty overthrew the Mongols. Korean general Yi Song-gye then led a revolt against the pro-Mongol king and seized control of the Korean government.

In 1392 General Yi assumed the crown and established the Yi dynasty, which lasted until 1910. The Yi dynasty maintained suzerain status with the Chinese Empire, however, which required

The Mongols, shown here during the medieval period with traditional wagons and huts, ruled Korea for over a century, beginning in A.D. 1259.

Korea to pay tribute to China in return for Korean independence. During the Yi dynasty Koreans adopted Confucianism—the teachings of Chinese philosopher Confucius—as the official state religion.

Japan first intruded into Korean affairs in 1592 and again in 1596. Japanese invaders commanded by General Toyotomi Hideyoshi tried to establish bases in Korea from which to attack China. Korea resisted Japan's aggression during a period that saw Korean admiral Yi Sun-sin invent the ironclad "turtle ships." These vessels enabled Yi to destroy most of the Japanese fleet.

But war with Japan so weakened China's Ming dynasty that it collapsed under attack from the north. In 1644 Manchurian invaders then established the Manchu or Chi'ing dynasty that ruled China until 1911. The Manchus overran Korea in 1647, forcing Korea once again to seek suzerain status. With its foreign relations controlled by the Manchu government in Peking (Beijing), Korea resisted opening itself to foreign trade and became known as the Hermit Kingdom.

Elder Brother

In 1866 the American trading vessel *General Sherman* dropped anchor in the Taedong River, in the northwestern area below Pyongyang. The Koreans attacked the ship and slaughtered the Americans. Five years later, the United States took its revenge. On June 10, 1871, U.S. Marines landed in Korea at the mouth of the Han River and seized command of the approaches to Seoul. Six marines and nine sailors earned Medals of Honor for this action, which eventually contributed to improved relations between Korea and the United States. The two nations signed an agreement on May 22, 1882, that granted trading rights and most favored nation status to the United States.

Korea's king viewed the United States as a nation too remote to pose a threat to Korean territory. He also saw Korea's new friendship with the United States as a shield against any unwanted pressure from China, Russia, and Japan.

With such ends in mind, the king commented, "We feel that America is to us as our Elder Brother."

At that time, the United States was neither able nor of a mind to involve itself in Asian affairs. But three score and eight years later, Americans would rush to the defense of a Korean nation once again victimized by invaders.

Under Japanese Rule

In 1894 a citizens' uprising against foreign involvement in Korean affairs prompted Korea to seek China's help in restoring order. Japan responded to China's intervention by sending troops to Korea to "protect Japanese interests." This ignited the Sino-Japanese War of 1894–1895. Japan won the war handily.

In 1860 Russia had extended its eastern boundary by seizing from China the Manchurian coastal area known as the Maritime Province. Following the Sino-Japanese conflict, Imperial Russia stood poised on the eleven-mile stretch of border that it shared with Korea. Between 1896 and 1904, the Russians secured mineral and timber rights in Korea. Russia then attempted to establish ports for its Far Eastern fleet in Masan and Mokpo on the Korean Straits. The Russians also tried but failed to divide Korea at the 39th parallel to provide a "buffer" between Russian territory and Japanese-controlled southern Korea. A dispute between Russia and Japan followed that led to the Russo-Japanese War of 1904–1905.

Chinese and Japanese troops collide during the Sino-Japanese War of 1894–1895. The Japanese won the conflict.

Japanese troops poise for action against the Russians during the Russo-Japanese War of 1904–1905. The Japanese won this second conflict easily.

Japan emerged the victor in its second war within a decade. The peace settlement that followed Russia's defeat cleared the way for Japan to annex Korea as a colony in 1910. Japan then began an ugly occupation of Korea that lasted for thirty-five brutal years. Under Japanese rule, Korean citizens were reduced to "haulers of water and hewers of wood."

In 1919 the Koreans staged a massive revolt involving 370,000 people, but the Japanese subdued the uprising swiftly. According to a Korean source, the Japanese killed 6,670 protesters, wounded 16,000, and jailed another 19,515. In April 1919, the Korean revolutionaries established a temporary government in Shanghai with Syngman Rhee—then exiled in the United States—as president.

Japan maintained its iron-handed control of Korea and later used the peninsula as a springboard for invading Manchuria in 1931. The Japanese turned occupied Manchuria into the puppet state of Manchukuo. In July 1937, Japanese troops crossed into China, setting off another Sino-Japanese war that would last for eight long and bloody years.

Inspired by dreams of becoming the major power in the Far East and western Pacific, Japan decided to neutralize its chief rival in the Pacific. Japan's sneak attack on the U.S. Pacific Fleet at Pearl Harbor, on December 7, 1941, would provoke America's entry into World War II and result in Japan's ultimate defeat. Along with multiple other losses, Japan would also lose dominion over Korea.

The Japanese used Korea as a launching-off place to invade China in what would become the second Sino-Japanese conflict in 1937. Here, Japanese troops occupy Shanghai in 1937.

Two Koreas

On August 8, 1945, less than a month before the formal Japanese surrender aboard the USS *Missouri* in Tokyo Bay on September 2, 1945, the Soviet Union declared war on Japan. The Soviets then invaded Korea on August 11 and 12. By so doing, the Soviets moved themselves in position to accept the surrender of Japanese forces in northern Korea.

Immediately following the surrender ceremonies in Tokyo, General of the Army Douglas MacArthur, Supreme Commander of Allied Powers (SCAP), issued General Order One. Included in the order were detailed instructions to Allied commanders for accepting the surrender of Japanese forces scattered about the Far East. The document had been prepared in Washington by the Army Staff's Strategy and Policy Group. It was next reviewed by top U.S. military and cabinet officials and approved by President Harry S. Truman. It was then coordinated with British and Soviet leaders. Regarding Korea, General Order One specified that Japanese forces north of the 38th parallel would surrender to the Soviets. Japanese forces south of the parallel would yield their arms to the Americans.

The United States viewed the 38th parallel in Korea as a temporary marker. The Soviets commenced at once to construct permanent fortifications along the parallel. An "iron curtain" clanged down across Korea, three months before Winston Churchill identified the "curtain" in a famous speech delivered in Fulton, Missouri.

For a time, the United States floundered about south of the parallel, lacking a sense of purpose or direction as to the future of Korea. Ill prepared to shore up a government and economy in collapse, the country wanted more than anything else to remove itself from Korea. In September 1947, the U.S. Joint Chiefs of Staff declared that Korea represented little of strategic importance to the United States. The question of Korean independence was then turned over to the United Nations for resolution.

Republic of Korea

Citizens in the north of Korea were already under the control of Soviet-trained Kim Il-sung. They refused to take part in UN attempts to reunite the north and the south as one independent nation. In May 1948, despite no cooperation from the north, elections were held in the south. Syngman Rhee was elected president of the Republic of Korea. The U.S. occupation ended on August 15, 1948, and the Republic of Korea (ROK) took its place among sovereign nations. The withdrawal of American troops commenced in September of that year.

Democratic People's Republic of Korea

The Soviets, however, held other ideas. Their defeat in the war with Japan in 1905 had denied them a friendly buffer state along their Far Eastern border. They saw in their occupation of northern Korea an opportunity to restore that buffer. In August 1945,

North Koreans were ruled by Soviet-trained Kim Il-sung while Syngman Rhee (above) was the elected president of South Korea.

Syngman Rhee

Syngman Rhee, the first president of the Republic of Korea, was born on April 26, 1875, in Hwanghae Province in what is now North Korea. His education for public life began in Seoul in 1897, where he converted to Christianity while in jail as a result of student political activities. Upon his release from jail, Rhee completed his education in the United States. He earned a B.A. from George Washington University, an M.A. from Harvard, and a Ph.D. in theology from Princeton.

Rhee returned to Korea in 1910 but was soon forced to flee to Hawaii to escape the consequences of continued revolutionary activities. He was elected president of the Korean Provisional Government in 1919. From 1920 through 1941, he attended annual meetings in Shanghai of his government-in-exile. Rhee openly criticized the United States for allowing Korea to be split at the 38th parallel after World War II, but his strong anticommunist views were always acceptable to Washington. He was elected president of the new South Korean state, the Republic of Korea, and took office on August 15, 1948.

When war came to Korea in 1950, Rhee became a cooperative ally at first. But he later disrupted peace talks by threatening to continue fighting alone until Korea was reunited. He continued to impede the peace process until July 1953, when a communist offensive forced ROK troops to withdraw six miles from the center of the UN lines near Kumsong.

Rhee remained the South Korean president until a student-led revolt in 1960 forced him to flee once more to Hawaii. He died in Hawaii on July 19, 1965.

Kim Il-sung

Marshal Kim Il-sung, North Korea's self-appointed "Great Leader," personally commanded the North Korean People's Army throughout the Korean War. He directed all combat operations by means of a Soviet-style "front" headquarters, similar to an American army field headquarters. Although Kim was supposedly also in command of Chinese "volunteers," the Chinese Communist forces probably took their orders from Peking (Beijing) rather than Pyongyang, the North Korean capital.

Born April 15, 1912, as Kim Song Ju, outside Pyongyang, he adopted the name Kim Il-sung after his uncle, who had disappeared following the Korean independence uprising in 1919. Japanese authorities described him as a bandit leader as late as 1945. He was also known to have served as a Soviet Army major during World War II (some say at Stalingrad).

Kim so endeared himself to the Soviets that they eventually selected him to serve as their man in North Korea. In 1946 he was unanimously elected chairman of the Provisional People's Committee for North Korea and head of the politburo of the Korean Labor Party. Kim became premier of the Democratic People's Republic of Korea (North Korea) on September 9, 1948. When the Korean War started on June 25, 1950, he further assumed the role of supreme military commander of the North Korea People's Army.

Kim Il-sung, the "Great Leader," continued to govern North Korea until his death in 1994, when he passed on his rule to Kim Jong Il, his son and North Korea's "Dear Leader."

---

the Soviets bypassed popular elections and installed Kim Il-sung as North Korea's new leader. The Soviet-sponsored Kim set himself at once to the task of eliminating political opponents.

Kim Il-sung quickly appointed Russian-trained Koreans to key government positions and created an Interim People's Committee. He patterned his government after the Marxist-Leninist (communist) government of his Soviet sponsors. Out of this emerged the Democratic People's Republic of Korea (DPRK) on September 9, 1948. Securely "buffered" in the east, the Soviets withdrew all their troops north of the Soviet-Korean border by December 26, 1948.

A Short Calm

In January 1950, during an address to the National Press Club in Washington, D.C., Secretary of State Dean Acheson described the U.S. defense line in the Far East:

> This defense perimeter runs along the Aleutians to Japan and then goes to the Ryukyus . . . from the Ryukyus to the Philippines. So far as the military security of other areas in the Pacific is concerned, it must be clear that no person can guarantee these areas against military attack.

The secretary's words excluded any mention of Korea and echoed clearly in the Kremlin.

UN forces withdraw from the North Korean capital of Pyongyang after the establishment of separate Koreas.

America's Main Task

The U.S. occupation of South Korea began showing signs of becoming a liability in early 1947. Pressed to save money by a shrinking postwar budget, the Joint Chiefs of Staff (JCS) proclaimed that the United States "has little strategic interest in maintaining the present [U.S.] troops and bases in Korea."

The JCS further indicated that in the event of any communist aggression that threatened American strategic interests in the Far East, "neutralization by air action would be more feasible and less costly than large scale ground operations."

In September 1947, the Soviets unexpectedly proposed withdrawing their troops from North Korea, if only the United States would do the same in South Korea. The U.S. government saw this as a chance to beat the budget crunch and exit Korea gracefully.

The next month, George F. Kennan, chairman of the State Department's Policy Planning Staff, summarized the department's views on Korea:

> There is no longer any real hope of a genuinely peaceful and free democratic development in that country. Its political life in the coming period is bound to be dominated by political immaturity, intolerance and violence. Where such conditions prevail, the communists are in their element. Therefore we cannot count on native forces to help hold the line against Soviet expansion. Since the territory is not of decisive strategic importance to us, our main task is to extricate ourselves without too great a loss of prestige.

In June 1950, the Soviet-sponsored Democratic People's Republic of Korea turned a greedy eye toward the Republic of Korea. Kim Il-sung, supported by a powerful, Soviet-trained-and-equipped army, entertained thoughts of reuniting the two Koreas. By then, only the 175 officers, 5 warrant officers, and 290 enlisted personnel composing the Korea Military Advisory Group (KMAG) remained in South Korea. In KMAG, U.S. support for the government of Syngman Rhee hardly compared with Soviet support for that of Kim Il-sung.

The calm that had settled over Korea after years of Japanese occupation and a world war was about to be shattered.

CHAPTER ONE

The First Month of War: Stand or Die!

The world has long known Korea as both the Hermit Kingdom of East Asia and the Land of the Morning Calm. On Sunday morning, June 25, 1950, four columns of North Korean soldiers swarmed across the 38th parallel into South Korea, thereby denying its isolation and shattering its calm.

The invading forces of the North Korean People's Army (NKPA), under the command of General Choe Yong-gun, comprised seven infantry divisions, one tank brigade, and thousands of supporting troops. In all, their forces totaled 135,000 men. The North Koreans claimed that their aggression was a "national defense" measure, necessary to counter an alleged "invasion" of their own country by units of the Republic of Korea Army (ROKA). South Korea strongly denied all such claims.

The United States had completed the formal withdrawal of its occupation forces from South Korea in June 1949. It left behind only that token group of five hundred military personnel known as the Korea Military Advisory Group (KMAG). Their mission was to complete the training of the Republic of Korea Army. Understandably, some members of the KMAG regarded this task as a "mission impossible."

The Americans hoped to make the ROKA strong enough to stand alone in defending its border against a possible attack from the north. At the same time, they did not want the South Koreans to grow so strong as to consider mounting an attack of their own. The United States, to curb any such thinking, decided against fur-

This photo clearly shows the rugged mountainous terrain along the 38th parallel that divided North and South Korea. The communists control the territory in the right background and the valley in the center distance.

nishing the ROKA with tanks, planes, and heavy weapons. This decision left South Korea at a huge disadvantage. On the eve of North Korean aggression, the Soviet-trained NKPA outnumbered the ROKA by some thirty-seven thousand troops. More important, the NKPA brought heavy metal to the mismatch: Soviet-supplied T-34 tanks, MiG-17 jet fighters, and an assortment of cannons and mortars.

Under cover of heavy rains and murky darkness, the NKPA moved relentlessly forward all along the 38th parallel, crushing what little resistance the ROK forces could muster. Approximately eighty-nine thousand crack troops attacked south in six tightly packed columns. The main assault came in the Uijongbu Corridor, an ancient invasion route used centuries earlier by the Mongol hordes of Kublai Khan. Although taken by complete surprise, the ROKs—many of whom were on weekend leave—met the North Koreans head-on, battling valiantly but vainly. Outnumbered five or six to one, and without suitable arms to challenge the onrushing armor of NK tanks, the ROKs collapsed quickly. Their forces scattered to the winds and withdrew hastily southward.

The World Reacts

News of the North Korean attack first reached officials in the United States at 2104 on Saturday, June 24, 1950 (actually 1004 the next day in Korea). The headlines in the Sunday morning

The North Koreans used Soviet-made tanks like this one when they invaded South Korea across the 38th parallel.

Military times are used throughout the book. This key, showing familiar A.M. and P.M. times paired with the corresponding time on the twenty-four-hour clock, may be helpful in learning the system.

A.M.	24	P.M.	24
1	0100	1	1300
2	0200	2	1400
3	0300	3	1500
4	0400	4	1600
5	0500	5	1700
6	0600	6	1800
7	0700	7	1900
8	0800	8	2000
9	0900	9	2100
10	1000	10	2200
11	1100	11	2300
12	1200	12	2400

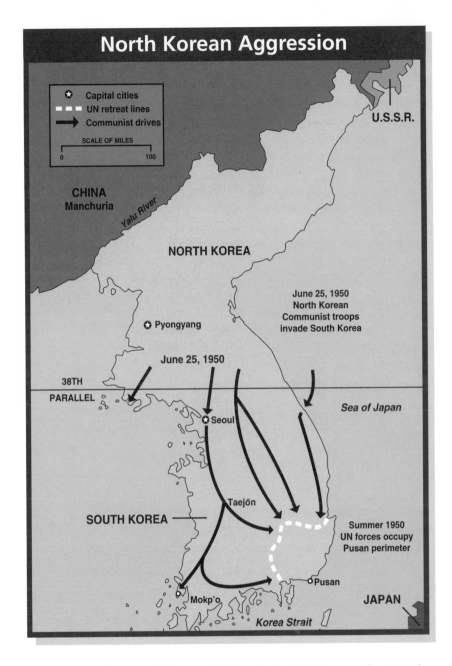

North Korean Aggression

Capital cities
UN retreat lines
Communist drives

SCALE OF MILES
0   100

U.S.S.R.

CHINA
Manchuria

Yalu River

NORTH KOREA

June 25, 1950
North Korean
Communist troops
invade South Korea

⊗ Pyongyang

June 25, 1950

38TH
PARALLEL

⊗ Seoul

Sea of Japan

Taejŏn

SOUTH KOREA

Summer 1950
UN forces occupy
Pusan perimeter

○ Pusan

Mokp'o

JAPAN

Korea Strait

newspapers featured the crash into Lake Michigan of a North-west Airlines DC-4. Media coverage of the invasion of South Korea amounted to little or nothing at that point. Similarly, in Tokyo, General Douglas MacArthur voiced little concern over North Korea's aggression, calling it only a probable "reconnaissance in force."

General MacArthur, hero of two world wars, then headed two military commands in Tokyo. He wore five stars and served as supreme commander of Allied powers (SCAP), as well as commander in chief of all American naval, air, and ground forces in the Far East (CINCFE). The outspoken general had already

General Douglas MacArthur

The many sides of General of the Army Douglas MacArthur—a towering figure among military giants—almost defy brief summation. Massive volumes on his legendary life tend only to show the need for another. But if a word sketch must suffice, William Manchester's introduction to his biographical subject in *American Caesar* surely ranks with the best in kind:

> He was a great thundering paradox of a man, noble and ignoble, inspiring and outrageous, arrogant and shy, the best of men and the worst of men, the most protean [changeable], most ridiculous, and most sublime. No more baffling, exasperating soldier ever wore a uniform. Flamboyant, imperious [lordly], and apocalyptic [suggestive of doom], he carried the plumage of a flamingo, could not acknowledge errors, and tried to cover up his mistakes with sly, childish tricks. Yet he was also endowed with great personal charm, a will of iron, and a soaring intellect. Unquestionably he was the most gifted man-at-arms this nation has produced. He was also extraordinarily brave. His twenty-two medals—thirteen of them for heroism—probably exceeded those of any other figure in American history.

Douglas MacArthur was born in Little Rock, Arkansas, on January 26, 1880, the third son of the famous general and holder of the Medal of Honor, Arthur MacArthur. He graduated from West Point at the top of his class in 1903. Promoted to brigadier general during World War I, MacArthur served with distinction as a brigade and division commander in the Champagne-Marne and St. Mihiel battles, and in the Meuse-Argonne sector. Twice wounded in action, he earned two Distinguished Service Crosses and seven Silver Stars for battlefield bravery.

MacArthur achieved fame in 1942 when he left the Philippines vowing "I shall return." Promoted to five-star rank and awarded the Medal of Honor by President Franklin D. Roosevelt in 1944, he returned to the Philippines in January 1945 and directed the liberation of the islands shortly thereafter.

MacArthur assumed command of U.S. Army Forces Far East in April 1945 and was appointed supreme commander of Allied powers in August 1945. In that capacity, he accepted the Japanese surrender aboard the battleship *Missouri* in Tokyo Bay on September 2, 1945.

Commanding the UN forces during the first months of the Korean War, MacArthur achieved his greatest victory at Inchon and successfully directed his forces in their northward drive to the Yalu River. When the Chinese entered the war in late November 1950, MacArthur began to disagree publicly with U.S. strategic policy. President Harry S. Truman judged these statements to be insubordination and relieved MacArthur of his command on April 11, 1951.

MacArthur promptly retired from the service and from public life. He died at Walter Reed Army Medical Center in Washington, D.C., on April 5, 1964.

Controversial general Douglas MacArthur played a major role during the Korean War.

boasted to John Foster Dulles regarding the developing Korean situation.

— "If Washington only will not hobble me," MacArthur told him, "I can handle it with one hand tied behind my back."

Dulles, an adviser to the U.S. secretary of state, had been stopping over in Tokyo after visiting Korea. His findings about the weaknesses of the ROK defenses caused Dulles to place less than full confidence in MacArthur's boast. Dulles cabled his misgivings to Secretary of State Acheson:

> TO SIT BY WHILE KOREA IS OVERRUN BY UNPROVOKED ARMED ATTACK WOULD START A DISASTROUS CHAIN OF EVENTS LEADING MOST PROBABLY TO WORLD WAR.

When Dulles arrived back in Washington, he told superiors that he had intended the use of U.S. air and naval forces only, not ground troops.

The news from Korea caught President Harry S. Truman out of town. He had flown to Kansas City, Missouri, the day before to spend a weekend in his hometown of Independence. Truman quickly authorized Secretary of State Acheson to act for him until he could return to the capital the next day. Acheson arranged at once for an emergency meeting of the United Nations Security Council in New York. The council, acting without the Soviet member present, called for an immediate withdrawal of North Korean troops from South Korea and requested the assistance of all member nations.

American Commitment

A three-hour flight back to Washington allowed President Truman time to reflect on the Korean incident. "I remembered how each time that the democracies failed to act it had encouraged the aggressors to go ahead," Truman recalled.

> Communism was acting in Korea just as Hitler, Mussolini, and the Japanese had acted ten, fifteen, and twenty years earlier. . . . If this was allowed to go unchallenged, it would mean a third world war. . . . It was also clear to me that the foundations and the principles of the United Nations were at stake unless this unprovoked attack on Korea could be stopped.

Back in Washington on June 27, President Truman authorized General MacArthur to support ROK resistance with available U.S. air and naval forces.

MacArthur acted at once to provide the authorized air support and quickly established a naval blockade of the North Korean coast. He then decided to fly into Suwon, south of Seoul, for a first-hand view of the military situation in South Korea. It was not good.

Adviser to the U.S. secretary of state during the start of the Korean War, John Foster Dulles was not as confident as MacArthur about a quick resolution to the conflict.

President Truman with Secretary of State Acheson during happier times. Truman was out of town when North Korea invaded the south, and Acheson was responsible for gathering statesmen for a meeting upon Truman's return.

Returning to his CINCFE headquarters in Tokyo, MacArthur dispatched a glum report to Washington on June 30:

> The only assurance for the holding of the present line, and the ability to regain later the lost ground [Seoul had fallen on June 28], is through the introduction of U.S. Ground Combat Forces into the Korean battle area. . . . If authorized, it is my intention to immediately move a United States Regimental Combat Team [RCT] to the reinforcement of the vital area discussed and to provide for a possible build-up to a two-division strength from the troops in Japan for an early counter-offensive.

Truman replied: "Your recommendation to move one RCT to combat area is approved. You will be advised later as to further build-up." Thus were American ground forces committed.

War Trumpet

The United States reacted quickly to the Korean crisis. On June 27, 1950, President Truman ordered all available U.S. naval and air forces in the Far East to help in the ROK Army's defense of its homeland. In New York, the United Nations fully supported the president's action and urged its member nations to join in the effort to throw back the North Korean invaders.

In Washington, D.C., the Senate Armed Services Committee geared up for what they perceived to be a major threat to world peace and democracy itself. They started an immediate call-up of reserve forces. Many of those called back to active duty had suffered and sacrificed greatly in World War II. It hardly seemed fair to send them off to war again. But no one ever said that war is fair.

On June 30, Congress authorized the activation of any or all reserve units, as needed, for a twenty-one-month period. On that same day, President Truman signed Public Law 599, a bill extending the Selective Service (the draft) for up to twenty-one months of active federal service. The bill also authorized the call-up of the National Guard and Reserves for a like period.

The trumpet of war again sounded across the land. And Americans rushed forth once more to answer its call.

William F. Dean

Major General William Frishe Dean became military governor of South Korea in October 1947. Dean assumed command of the 24th Infantry Division, based on the southern Japanese island of Kyushu in October 1949.

In June 1950, the 24th Infantry Division became the first American ground combat unit committed to action in the Korean War. Dean arrived in Korea on July 3, 1950, and established headquarters at Taejon. General Walton H. Walker, Eighth U.S. Army commander, assigned to Dean's division the task of delaying the North Korean advance until additional American troops could be deployed. The division suffered heavy losses and Dean personally led tank-killer teams against attacking enemy T-34 tanks.

General Dean became separated from his men when his division withdrew from Taejon on July 20. He was captured by the North Koreans on August 25 and spent the rest of the war as their prisoner. His country later honored his conduct in combat and as a prisoner of war by awarding him the Medal of Honor.

Born in Carlyle, Illinois, on August 1, 1899, Dean graduated from the University of California at Berkeley in 1922. He was commissioned a second lieutenant in the Army reserve in 1922. As a major general in Europe during World War II, he commanded the 44th Infantry Division in combat and won a Distinguished Service Cross for bravery. General Dean retired from active service on October 31, 1955, and died on August 25, 1981.

An army historian would later write: "General MacArthur quite clearly tipped the balance of favor of troop commitment."

The Fall of Seoul

Seventy-two hours after the outbreak of hostilities, the South Korean capital of Seoul fell before the rapid advance of NKPA tanks and infantry. Many on the scene compared their sweeping attack to the blitzkrieg (lightning war) executed by Hitler's Panzer divisions in the Second World War. Without tanks to counter those of the NKPA, the ROK defeat became not a question of if but rather of when.

Oddly, Major General W. Lynn Roberts, KMAG commander and a former tank officer in World War II, dismissed the need to supply the ROKs with tanks. He noted that the Korean terrain "was not good tank country." An old tanker should have known better.

As a result of Roberts's error in judgment, the ROKs faced off against the crushing assault of Soviet-built T-34 tanks armed only with bazookas and satchel charges. The small 2.36-inch bazooka rockets bounced off the armored tanks like hailstones off a tea kettle. A few well-placed explosives under tank treads, and a handful of grenades stuffed into open tank hatches, helped to slow the NKPA advance. But the cost in lives was high, the outcome of battle inevitable.

The fall of Seoul left little doubt that a *real* war was going on—and that the United States was *really* in it.

Task Force Smith

On July 1, 1950, 440 soldiers of the 24th Infantry Division's First Battalion, 21st Infantry Regiment, boarded six C-54 Skymasters (troop/cargo-carrying airplanes) at Itazuki air base in Japan and shuttled into Pusan airfield. Named for its commanding officer, Lieutenant Colonel Charles B. Smith, the group became known as Task Force Smith. This task force drew the dubious honor of being the first U.S. unit to fight in Korea.

Two days after the First Battalion's arrival, Major General William F. Dean flew into Taejon airstrip to take command of the 24th Infantry Division. Taejon, South Korea's sixth largest city, is located one hundred miles south of Seoul. General Dean planned to make it his command post.

Meanwhile, the NKPA pressed southward unchecked. Inchon fell to the North Koreans on July 3.

Early on the morning of July 5, the soldiers of Task Force Smith moved into selected defensive positions about three miles south of Osan, a village located between Seoul and Taejon on the Seoul-Pusan highway. Their role in General Dean's tactical

North Korean prisoners of war are guarded by South Korean soldiers.

plan was to block and delay the NKPA advance. Dean needed desperately to buy time until he could bolster his entire defensive posture by bringing up two infantry regiments from Pusan—the 21st and the even more recently arrived 34th.

At 0700, the NKPA's Fourth Division moved against the Osan defenders. The attackers drew strong fire from Smith's supporting artillery, 75mm recoilless rifles, and 2.36-inch rocket launchers. Despite the barrage, thirty T-34 medium tanks crashed through American defenses. North Korean infantry followed. At great personal cost, the NK troops forced the American soldiers to withdraw in scattered disorder in only a few hours.

News of this shocking defeat spread quickly throughout the rest of the 24th Division and severely affected morale. As one soldier recalled:

> News of the delaying action at Osan had an unhealthy effect on the rank and file of the 24th Division. . . . It planted a doubt in many minds about the effectiveness of our tactics and weapons . . . [and] swollen by rumor . . . the doubt ate like a cancer into the combat morale of all troops moving to the front.

The First to Land

The U.S. Marines have long prided themselves on being the nation's first to fight. In the early days of the Korean War, the marines wasted little time in establishing still another first. Under a mantle of darkness on the night of July 11–12, 1950, the marines landed in Korea.

A marine officer and four enlisted men from the cruiser *Juneau* slipped ashore south of the east coast of Songjin in a whale boat off the destroyer *Mansfield*. Packing two 60-pound explosive charges, they worked their way inland to a nearby railroad tunnel and rigged the explosives. The landing party returned safely to the *Juneau* and later learned that the next train set off the charges and blocked the tunnel. The marines took pride in having become the first Americans to land in *North* Korea.

Their mission fell far short of the major amphibious operations for which the marines became famous during World War II, but it was a start.

Four days earlier on July 7, the First Provisional Marine Brigade, under Brigadier General Edward A. Craig, began forming around the Fifth Marines at Camp Pendleton and Marine Air Group 33 (MAG-33) at El Toro, California. On July 14, only one week after it had been organized and twelve days after MacArthur had requested it, the brigade of 6,534 marines boarded ship in San Diego. General Clifton B. Cates, the commandant of the Marine Corps, flew out from Washington to wish them well and watch them sail for Korea.

The survivors of Task Force Smith reassembled several days later in Taejon. Five officers and 148 enlisted men failed to return and were declared missing in action. A monument still marks the site of their ill-fated stand at Osan.

A Battle Against Time

After losing Osan, General Dean turned his attention south along th Seoul-Pusan road to the town of Pyongtaek, the next most likely spot to defend. On July 6, he called on the First Battalion of the 24th Infantry Division's 34th Infantry Regiment to stop or delay the relentless North Korean advance. He asked too much for one battalion to deliver. Lacking artillery support and communications, the First Battalion performed poorly and was overrun by enemy tanks and superior forces. The American soldiers pulled back quickly to Chonan.

First Battalion commander Lieutenant Colonel Harold L. "Red" Ayres later wrote:

> Dean and Barth [Brigadier General George B. Barth, 24th Division artillery commander] acted as if they were deploying corps against numerically inferior forces instead of three weak, poorly-armed battalions against divisions of well-armed and well-trained and well-supported NKPA forces. . . . Dean's impression that this [Pyongtaek] was a strong position with its left flank secured by the Yellow Sea was erroneous.

The next day, the 34th Regiment's Third Battalion, which had survived Osan, put up a stiffer fight at Chonan, until nearly trapped and almost wiped out. Two-thirds of the battalion was killed or surrendered. Only the cover of a smoke screen from white phosphorus shells laid down by the 63rd Artillery Battalion enabled 175 of them to escape.

And so it went down paths of inglorious defeat, south through Chochiwon to the Kum River defense line. The 19th and 34th Infantry Regiments of the 24th Division paused at the river and attempted another delaying action.

The war then became a race against time. Its outcome would depend on whether reinforcements would arrive before the NKPA could run the Americans right off the peninsula.

The week of July 10–18 saw the 25th Infantry Division move into Korea from bases in Japan. On July 12, the First Cavalry Division began staging in Yokohama for a similar move. Lieutenant General Walton H. Walker arrived in Korea on July 13 to establish headquarters at Taegu for the Eighth U.S. Army (EUSA). Two days later, the 29th Regimental Combat Team departed Okinawa and steamed full ahead toward the besieged peninsula. Help was on the way. But would it arrive in time?

On July 18, lead elements of the First Cavalry Division landed unopposed at Pohang on Korea's east coast. General Walker then appealed to the 24th Infantry Division to hold on at Taejon for two days while he deployed the First Cavalry. This they managed, but just barely. Taejon fell on July 20. And in the fog of war that blanketed the fighting, General William F. Dean, 24th Infantry Division commander, vanished.

(During the withdrawal from Taejon, Dean became separated from his unit and suffered injuries from a fall down a hill while trying to avoid capture. He managed to dodge the enemy for thirty-six days but was finally caught on August 25. Dean then spent nearly three years as America's highest-ranking prisoner of war. For his model conduct and "unbreakable" spirit while a POW, President Truman later awarded Dean the Medal of Honor for personal heroism.)

On July 27, General MacArthur flew into Taegu on the *Bataan*, his private airplane, to confer with General Walker. He expressed concern to Walker regarding any further troop withdrawals. The sum of his talk with Walker emphasized that the Eighth Army must hold in place. MacArthur's grand strategy stood at risk. He wanted no Dunkirk-type evacuation of troops from Korea. General Walker got the message.

After the initial shock of the invasion, U.S. forces tried to help the South Koreans regain lost time. U.S. fighter jets (like the one at left) and air raids over strategic targets, such as this bombing of a North Korean oil refinery, were examples of U.S. tactical aid.

Forsaking his earlier plans to withdraw the First Cavalry and 25th Divisions to the Naktong River, Walker ordered his field commanders to remain in place until reinforcements arrived. Notes recorded in the 25th Division's command post journal by division commander Major General William B. Kean captured the highlights of General Walker's "pep talk":

> We are fighting a battle against time. There will be no more retreating, withdrawal, or readjustment of the lines or any other terms you choose. There is no line behind us to which we can retreat. Every unit must counterattack to keep the enemy in a state of confusion and off-balance. There will be no Dunkirk [evacuation of British and French troops from European continent at Dunkirk, France, during May 26–June 4, 1940], there will be no Bataan [surrender of U.S. and Philippine defenders of Bataan Peninsula, Luzon, P.I., to Japanese invaders, on April 8, 1941, after three months of fierce fighting]. A retreat to Pusan would be one of the greatest butcheries in history. We must fight until the end. Capture by these people is worse than death itself. We will fight as a team. If some of us must die, we will die fighting together. Any man who gives ground may be personally responsible for the death of thousands of his comrades. . . . I want everybody to understand that we are going to hold this line. We are going to win.

Walker's grim instructions became famous—or infamous—as his "stand-or-die" order.

CHAPTER TWO

Pusan Perimeter: Hanging On

Before MacArthur's visit to Taegu, General Walker's strategy had called for a gradual withdrawal to the Naktong River. The Naktong presented a natural and more realistic line of resistance. To Walker's staff of officers (and probably to Walker himself), it seemed silly to stand and defend positions that had already been infiltrated and flanked by the NKPA. Whether Walker tried to hold the line as ordered by MacArthur remains unclear. He appeared to turn his head from continuing withdrawals by the First Cavalry and 25th Infantry Divisions. And again when the 24th Infantry Division followed suit. Did looking the other way signify his approval? Subsequent events quickly stripped the answer of any practical value.

The NKPA continued to advance in all sectors. Under enormous pressure, the Eighth U.S. Army—which included all ROK and other UN forces—pulled back into a final, desperate perimeter defense line.

The Naktong River formed most of its western boundary. The perimeter stretched a hundred miles from north to south, running east to west another fifty miles. It was further bound by mountains in the north, extending to the Sea of Japan in the east. In the south, the Straits of Korea added a fourth side to the rectangle. The stage was now set for the battle of Naktong Perimeter—perhaps better known to the world as the Pusan Perimeter.

On August 2, the First Provisional Marine Brigade from Camp Pendleton, California, arrived in Korea. The brigade became "blooded" on the night of August 3-4, when three trigger-happy "ground-pounders" (infantry troopers) wounded three of their

(Right) A color guard of South Korean soldiers stands ready to welcome U.S. Marines into South Korea. (Above) Railroad bridges span the Naktong River. The river was a natural boundary for North and South Korean troops to face off. In this picture, smoke from artillery rises from a village (left center).

own. Not a great beginning. Their lack of discipline earned the wrath of Brigadier General Edward A. Craig, brigade commander and Navy Cross winner on Guam during World War II. Marine Corps historian J. Robert Moskin described him as being "furious." One can only wonder how he felt about the brigade's next encounter.

On August 6, two marines of G Company, Third Battalion, Fifth Marines, were wounded by rifle fire from two U.S. soldiers near Chindong-ni. The army riflemen had not received word that marines had arrived to help F Company of the Fifth Infantry Regiment hold Hill 342. The marines' first days in Korea might well have inspired cartoonist Walt Kelly's Pogo to say, "We have met the enemy and he is us!"

Task Force Kean

The marines' war in Korea began in earnest on the morning of August 7, eight years to the day since their historic landing on Guadalcanal. The marine brigade linked up with the army's 35th Infantry Regiment and Fifth Regimental Combat Team (RCT) to form Task Force Kean (named for the commander of the 25th Infantry Division). The newly formed unit was then ordered to launch the first American counterattack of the six-week-old war.

The Eighth Army's attack plan called for the recapture of Chinju, followed by a sweep north to the Kum River. Three roads led to the first objective. EUSA assigned a regiment to each road. The 35th Regiment on the north prepared to move from Chungam-ni in a westward attack through Muchon-ni and on through to Chinju. Taking up positions at Chindong-ni on the coast, the Fifth RCT was to strike inland past Kogan-ni and then join up with the 35th at Muchon-ni. The marines were to follow the Fifth RCT, then slice off on the coast road near Kogan-ni in the southwest. Striking through Kosong and Sachon, they would press on to Chinju in an upward thrust from the south.

U.S. troops debark from a ship somewhere in Korea. The United States hoped to supplement and guide South Korean troops, not take over the conflict.

Hill 342

Second Lieutenant John H. Cahill and Sergeant Lee Buettner became the first marines to come under enemy ground fire when fifty-two men of G Company moved up the steep slopes of Hill 342. The North Koreans surrounded the hill and attacked in force, killing three marines and wounding eight others. Only thirty-seven of the original fifty-two marines reached the top of the hill. Later, an attempt to air drop ammunition and water to the embattled soldiers and marines went astray and landed in enemy territory. Soldiers of the NKPA's Sixth Division struck again just before dawn on August 8. Fierce hand-to-hand fighting erupted, but the Americans held on until relieved by D Company of the Fifth Marines. Cahill's platoon suffered total losses of six dead and twelve wounded. The next day, D Company added eight dead and twenty-eight wounded to the totals, before turning the hill over to the army's 24th Infantry Regiment.

While G and D companies staved off the North Koreans on Hill 342, H Company, Third Battalion, Fifth Marines, also came under enemy attack on nearby Hill 255. Pinned down by grenades and machine-gun fire, the marines under Captain Joseph C. Fegan Jr. froze in place. When his First and Third platoons failed to mount an attack, Fegan himself took over the assault. Corporal Melvin James joined his skipper, leading a BAR (Browning automatic rifle) attack against the enemy's left flank.

A U.S. Marine machine-gun crew digs in for the night in Korea.

He managed to rescue six wounded marines in the process. Not to be outdone by James, Technical Sergeant Ray Morgan and Private First Class Donald Terrio assailed the enemy's right flank and knocked out two machine guns. The marines of H Company went on to secure the hill the next morning, but only after paying a price of six dead and thirty-two wounded.

Marines Press On

Following their attack plan, Lieutenant Colonel George R. Newton's First Battalion, Fifth Marines, struck to the south, clearing the important road junction at Tosan and seizing control of Hill 308. The Second Battalion, Fifth Marines, commanded by Lieutenant Colonel Harold S. Roise, then moved through Newton's troops and took the lead on the road to Kosong. The NKPA waited for the marines to enter the narrow Taedabok Pass, nine miles north of Kosong, then ambushed them with a hail of automatic weapons fire from the high ground. Lieutenant Colonel Robert D. Taplett's Third Battalion, fresh from the fighting on Hill 342, detoured around the pass and helped to clear it the next day. The marines picked up the pace and pressed boldly on toward Kosong.

Marines Denied

August 12 brought more heavy fighting, as the First Battalion, Fifth Marines, moved through Kosong and approached Changchon on their way to Sachon. After driving the enemy back twenty-two miles in four days, the marines expected to reach Sachon—about eight miles south of their main objective of Chinju—the next day. The North Koreans again set up an ambush and a huge firefight broke out, continuing through the afternoon and into the evening. Marine Corsair fighter-bombers struck at the enemy, allowing the marine infantry to secure three hills that straddled the road, two on the south side and one on the north. This was as close as they got to Chinju.

Earlier that day, Taplett's Third Battalion had been whisked back to Chindong-ni following an enemy attack that all but destroyed two army artillery battalions. They arrived at dusk and immediately threw the enemy off the first ridge to the north, overrunning a second ridge before 1000 the next day. With the brigade now split between two fronts twenty-five miles apart, the First and Second Battalions at Changchon were ordered to withdraw.

But before they could carry out those orders, the North Koreans attacked and overran the Third Platoon of B Company that night and forced the marines to fight their way off Hill 202. When they finally made it off the hill, a squad at a time, their

Close Air Support

Throughout the fighting, pilots of the First Marine Air Wing supported their ground-pounding brothers with surgical strikes from the air. Flying World War II Corsairs off the carriers *Sicily* and *Badoen Strait* that lay close inshore, they flew sortie (a single flight by a single plane) after sortie, patrolling the roads ahead as well as the surrounding terrain.

The air and ground forces worked so well together that it became common for aircraft to arrive on scene within minutes of receiving a call. Some Corsairs made it a practice to circle above their troops to enable a quicker response when called upon for "services." This practice met with lots of approval from the troops below.

On August 11, four Corsairs from Marine Fighter Squadron 323 surprised a long string of vehicles comprising about two hundred trucks, jeeps, and motorcycles of the NKPA's 83rd Motorcycle Regiment on the road to Kosong. They quickly demonstrated the meaning of "close air support," raking the long line of vehicles with a withering strafing attack.

On a second strafing run, enemy small-arms fire brought down two of the Corsairs. Nothing, it seemed, came without paying a price. But news of the action brought another flight of marine Corsairs and air force F-51 Mustangs to the scene. They completed the deadly artistry of the first four.

Advancing ground forces later discovered 31 trucks, 24 jeeps, and 45 motorcycles destroyed or abandoned. The enemy suffered further losses of some 200 men plus much ammunition and other equipment. Not a bad tally for a few minutes on the job.

U.S. Corsairs like this one provided vital air support to ground troops in Korea.

losses totaled twelve dead, eighteen wounded, and eight missing in action (MIA). Because their withdrawal was already late, B Company's request to search for their MIAs was denied by Brigade. The denial left the men bitter. Marines do not relish leaving their own behind.

Full Circle

While the marines moved against the enemy with fair success on the left prong of the three-pronged attack on Chinju, the army's 35th Regiment and Fifth RCT met with stiff resistance in their sectors. The 35th struck out boldly at first in the north. It destroyed an important North Korean position and then mounted a rapid advance on Muchon-ni. But when the Fifth RCT tried to move in that direction, heavy sniper fire and 110-degree heat stopped their advance before they could link up with the 35th. Both units became stalled at this point and advanced no farther.

The North Koreans had attacked at daybreak that day and had pretty much destroyed the 555th (Triple Nickel) and the 90th Field Artillery units near Pongam-ni. Stripped of artillery support, the army infantry regiments fell into disarray and needed help from Taplett's marines to withdraw. The Fifth Marines on the left flank were then ordered back from their hard-won positions, and the first American counterattack collapsed.

When the battle ended, Task Force Kean stood at about the same place it had occupied at the start. Despite having pulled back, the men of the task force could draw some satisfaction in knowing that their efforts had halted the North Korean offensive.

First Battle of Naktong Bulge

Elements of the crack North Korean Fourth Division started crossing the Naktong River at various points on August 6. Following a failed attempt to dislodge them from Cloverleaf Hill and Obong-ni Ridge by the army's Task Force Hill (comprising units of the Second and 24th Divisions), General Walker again called on the marines. The Fifth Marines moved into position from Miryang and "jumped off" against Obong-ni Ridge at 0735 on August 17. At the same time, two infantry regiments, the 19th and the 24th, struck from the northeast, while part of the 21st Infantry Regiment blocked off the south.

The marines moved westward in a frontal assault under covering fire by the Ninth Regimental Combat Team. Obong-ni Ridge, located about three miles east of the "bulge" in the river, stands 300–450 feet high and stretches for a mile and a half along the south side of the Yongsan-Naktong road. If all went as planned, the marines would first recapture the ridge line, then lay down covering fire for the Ninth RCT's move on Cloverleaf Hill on the north side of the road.

Tired U.S. troops withdraw from Yongsan after being badly beaten back by the North Koreans.

Lieutenant Colonel Roise's Second Battalion spearheaded the assault. Owing to a series of flukes, his troopers took on heavy casualties. To begin with, a shortage of transportation caused the brigade to arrive late at the Miryang staging area. The shortage also adversely affected the artillery preparation normally used to "soften up" an objective. A mix-up with army units on the marines' right led to a lack of flank support. Finally, an air strike from offshore carriers arrived fifteen minutes late, allowing the marine Corsairs only half the time scheduled to work over the enemy positions. Many of their well-entrenched positions escaped undamaged from both artillery and aerial attacks.

Roise, his battalion short a full rifle company and vastly outnumbered by the NKPA, sent D and E companies abreast in an uphill advance. Caught in open terrain by machine-gun and mortar fire, they fought bravely but paid a high price. By noon, mauled and staggering after four hours of fighting, the Second Battalion faltered and fell back. Their losses by then numbered 23 dead and 119 wounded. Fifth Regiment commander Lieutenant Colonel Raymond L. Murray ordered Lieutenant Colonel Newton to move his First Battalion through the stalled and bloodied Second Battalion and pursue the attack on the heavily defended ridge line.

The First Battalion passed on through at 1300 and was greeted by more machine-gun and mortar fire. Much of the devastating enemy fire originated from the Cloverleaf vicinity. Murray then convinced the Ninth RCT of the need to attack Cloverleaf right away, instead of waiting for the marines to establish a base of fire on Obong-ni. They obliged by moving out against Cloverleaf at 1600. The attack came after the 24th Division's artillery had softened the hill with all the firepower it could muster, including V-T (variable-timed) shells that exploded in the air over the enemy foxholes. Proof that the artillery did its job came when the Ninth RCT secured Cloverleaf quite easily. The North Koreans lucky enough to live through the artillery barrage abandoned the hill and hightailed it to the rear.

Back on Obong-ni, the marines still found the taking of the ridge bordering on impossible. The fighting kept on hot and heavy until 1900, when a welcome lull afforded them a chance to dig in for the night. They now held the northern end of the ridge. At 2200, the NKs started lobbing in mortar rounds on A Company, tied to B Company on its right flank, open on its left. White phosphorus shells found and destroyed A Company's mortar section. A green flare lit the sky overhead at 0230, signaling the start of a North Korean attack. Under a blanket of automatic fire, the enemy split the two companies and forced A Company back down into

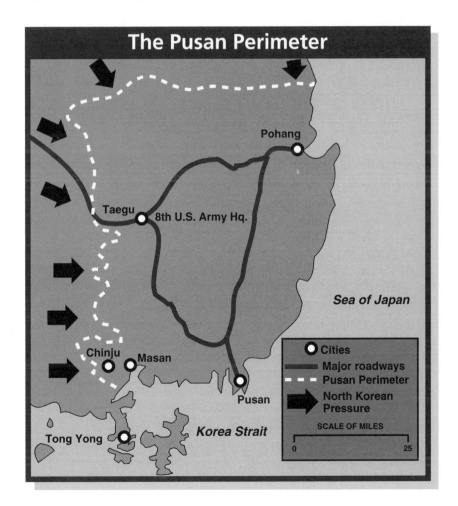

The Pusan Perimeter

The 24th Division moves up to the firing line. This division hammered Obong-ni Ridge with artillery fire, allowing other battalions to advance.

the draw. Marine artillery opened up on the NKs and prevented their further advance. Their attack fizzled out by dawn. B Company still held in place.

A Company pulled itself together and struck back at 0700. Acts of courage became the order of the day. Private First Class Harold Twedt, a BAR-man, stormed and destroyed two NK machine guns before he was killed. Captain John P. Kelley, a marine Corsair pilot, threaded the needle fifty yards in front of the advancing A Company. His 500-pound bomb hit a nest of four enemy machine guns with pinpoint accuracy.

The explosion shook the entire hill, killing one marine, but wiping out the deadly guns. A and B companies picked up the tempo of the attack, seizing control of hills 117, 147, and 153 in quick succession. By midafternoon, marines of the First Battalion, Fifth Regiment, owned all of Obong-ni Ridge.

On August 18, Lieutenant Colonel Taplett's Third Battalion moved against the marines' next objective. With G Company on the right flank and H on the left, they met only light resistance and reached the crest of Hill 207 at 1237. The defenders of Hill 311, the marines' final objective, put up a stiffer fight but finally abandoned the hill during the night. The Third Battalion secured the hill on the morning of August 19, marking the end of the First Battle of Naktong Bulge.

The remnants of the highly regarded Fourth NK Division swarmed back across the Naktong in panic while American artillery, mortars, and aircraft pursued them with killing fire. Lynn Montross and Nicholas A. Canzona wrote in their book *The Pusan Perimeter*, "Victory turned into slaughter when the Brigade supporting arms concentrated on the masses of Communists plunging into the river." Their blood turned the river red. North Korea now knew the color of defeat.

ROK Action at Pohang

Action continued unabated in the northeast corner of the Naktong (Pusan) Perimeter. With superior numbers, the NK Fifth and 12th Divisions all but surrounded the ROK Third Division on August 10 and forced it back to the sea at Pohang. The U.S. Navy managed to move the ROK division offshore before the city fell to the NKs. A quick redeployment of the Third Division to a landing spot south of the NK salient followed. The Third then teamed up with the ROK Eighth and Capital Divisions. Together, on August 20, they recaptured Pohang and destroyed the NK 12th Division in a highly satisfying joint effort.

Battle of Bowling Alley

About fifteen miles northeast of Taegu, the temporary seat of the ROK government, still another battle raged. This one involved Brigadier General Whitey Paik's First ROK Division. Because of massive NK forces gathering for a drive on the city, General Walker felt obliged to rush Brigadier General Mike Michaelis's 27th Infantry Regiment to help Paik's outmanned division. Walker, by then, looked upon the 27th as his "fire brigade." He had recently shown his appreciation to Michaelis by promoting him to flag rank. The new general was about to earn his keep. While the fighting for Ubong-ni reached a peak to the southwest of them, the 27th Infantry took up position in Tabu-dong Corridor. The main north-south road bisected the corridor located due north of Taegu—a valley about a mile long and contained on both sides by a string of rugged mountains: a virtual bowling alley (as it was to be dubbed later). Michaelis moved up a company of M-26 tanks and two artillery battalions to match up with the T-34 tanks and artillery of the People's 13th Division in front of him. With his regiment blocking passage at the south end of the valley, and Paik's First Division defending the high ground on his flanks, a strange kind of "bowling match" began shortly after dark that night. Seven days of bizarre fighting followed.

Iron Mike's Wolfhounds

Colonel John "Iron Mike" Michaelis, regimental commander of the Wolfhounds of the 27th Regiment, brought courage, experience, and a gift for plain speaking to the Korean battlefield. The outstanding, twice-wounded commander of a battalion in the 502nd Airborne Regiment during World War II spoke frankly about the army's failure to prepare his soldiers for combat. In an interview with the *Saturday Evening Post*, Michaelis described the shortcomings he found in the Wolfhounds when he arrived in Korea:

> In peacetime training, we've gone for too damn much folderol [trivia]. We've put too much stress on information and education and not enough stress on rifle marksmanship and scouting and patrolling and the organization of a defensive position. These kids of mine have all the guts in the world and I can count on them to fight. But when they started out, they couldn't shoot. They didn't know their weapons. They have not had enough training in plain, old-fashioned musketry [the use of small arms].

Michaelis returned to the scene of former battles in 1971 as a general officer and commander of U.S. forces in Korea.

The North Koreans set the table for an attack with a heavy artillery and mortar barrage. When the preparatory fire lifted, two T-34 tanks and a mobile 76mm gun cranked down the road, followed by infantry in trucks and on foot. The lead tank advanced without firing, while the second tank fired any which way at random. American bazooka teams moved into position and waited for the tanks to draw close. Then Bang!-Whoosh!-Boom! Bang! Whoosh!-Boom! At precisely the right moment, the 3.5-inch rocket teams launched their deadly missiles and took out the second tank. Two direct hits on the lead tank turned out to be duds. But the scared crew members bailed out of the escape hatches and ran off anyway, perhaps with thoughts of delayed-action explosives on their minds. At the same time, Michaelis's Eighth Artillery zeroed in on the NKs, wiping out the 76mm gun, two trucks, and more than a hundred foot soldiers. The sight of this destruction persuaded two more T-34s to turn around and return to the safety of its own lines. This ended the first night's activities. One down, six to go.

Each of the next six nights started with an NK barrage of artillery and mortar shells aimed straight down the road, plainly intended to search out and destroy Michaelis's M-26 tanks at the south end. The NKs would then follow up with an attempted

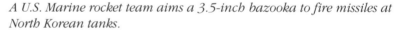

A U.S. Marine rocket team aims a 3.5-inch bazooka to fire missiles at North Korean tanks.

tank-infantry advance down the narrow corridor. From the vantage point of the GIs at the end of the valley, they could see bright flashes when the big guns fired off. And they could follow the paths of the incoming artillery shells, clearly visible red balls hurtling toward them in the night sky. The sounds of the big guns going off, and the thunderous explosions of the shells when they hit, bounced off the mountains and echoed back and forth across the valley. Witnessing the nightly show, the GIs began to think of the flaming projectiles as giant bowling balls, the mile-long stretch of straight road as a huge bowling alley. They were the pins.

From their well-entrenched positions, the Americans withstood every NK attempt to pass through the valley and move on to Taegu. Artillery and mortar fire played a key role in their defense. On the night of August 21-22 alone, the American gunners inflicted more than thirteen hundred casualties on the North Koreans. It finally dawned on the NKs that they were not going to make it through the valley. They needed to change their tactics before they lost a whole division. To this end, the NK 13th Division—joined then by the NK First Division—slipped through Paik's ROK division in the mountains during the night. The NK divisions, now behind Michaelis's 27th Regiment, penetrated to within nine miles of Taegu by noon on August 22. The North Koreans had used this tactic successfully at the Kum River and Taejon. But that was then. The tide of battle was shifting.

That afternoon, the NKs attacked along a five-mile stretch of the main supply road, then moved against elements of the U.S. Army's 23rd Infantry Regiment, eight miles from Taegu. But this time the good guys would prevail. Air force, navy, and Australian planes teamed up and delivered a knockout blow to the enemy holed up in the ridge line east of the road. Foot soldiers of the 23rd Infantry cleaned up what remained of the NK divisions the next morning. The Battle of Bowling Alley ended.

Second Battle of Naktong Bulge

As August drew to a close, ninety-eight thousand North Korean troops assembled along the Naktong (Pusan) Perimeter for a final, all-out assault on Pusan. For the second time in less than a month, the North Koreans crossed the Naktong River and occupied the Bulge area. This action signaled the start of the NKs' last major offensive in an attempt to drive to the sea.

They attacked in force and in unison all along the perimeter. Despite growing increasingly tired and hungry owing to their continuing advances and extended supply lines, the North Koreans fought savagely. Their most dangerous penetration, in the view of General Walker, came at the Bulge. Against the army's newly arrived Second Infantry Division, the NK Ninth Division

(Right) Fresh U.S. Marines, newly arrived at the supply port of Pusan, get ready to be moved up to the front lines. (Above) Marines aim a howitzer against North Korean troops.

had smashed a hole eight miles deep and six miles wide into their defense line. General Walker answered their threat by once again calling on the marines.

At 1330 on September 1, the First Marine Brigade boarded trucks and headed toward their staging area at Miryang for the second time. Two days later, D and E companies of Lieutenant Colonel Roise's Second Battalion advanced westward from Yongsan under tank and artillery support and stopped the enemy cold.

Less than two hours later, A and B companies of Lieutenant Colonel Newton's First Battalion moved up from south of the Yongsan-Naktong road. Forced to wade through several hundred yards of knee-deep rice paddies, the marines became unwilling targets for enemy small-arms fire.

Still, at 1100, they managed to mount a fierce attack on the ridge ahead. The marines made such frightful sounds that a company of North Koreans fled in terror from their foxholes on the forward slope. Advancing marines cut them down with automatic and rifle fire, allowing A Company to take the high ground along the ridge top. Marine Corsairs pounded the NKs in front of the First Battalion and sent them scurrying in retreat.

Meanwhile, marine tanks held a turkey shoot on the road, knocking out five NK tanks. Nightfall found the Second Battalion two miles west of Yongsan, where they had started. But again the price came high. The Second Battalion sustained losses of eighteen dead and seventy-seven wounded, most of the losses belonging to D Company.

With an eye to the Second's casualties, regimental commander Murray moved his Third Battalion through their positions. Along with the First Battalion, the Third then advanced another four thousand yards before digging in for the night.

The next day, September 5, rain and fog greeted the marines as they continued to push ahead. Another kind of greeting in the form of North Korean artillery and mortar fire poured down on them from Obong-ni Ridge up ahead, an old battleground revisited. Murray planned to reoccupy the ridge line while the army's Ninth Infantry regiment was taking back Cloverleaf Hill.

But an NK counterattack led by T-34 tanks and armored troop carriers turned the marines' attention to the road. The T-34s caught two marine M-26s by surprise and knocked out both of them.

A U.S. M-26 tank is poised to attack the North Koreans as they attempt to cross the Naktong River.

(Above) A North Korean who was taken prisoner after the fighting at Naktong. (Right) These innocent casualties of war were killed when caught in the line of fire.

Fortunately for the marines, D Company rushed in their 3.5-inch rockets and took out the two T-34s and an armored carrier.

Army and marine artillery and mortar fire finally shut down the NK attack. The action to take back the Bulge in effect rendered two NK divisions useless.

On the night of September 5–6, the army's Second Division relieved the marines' positions. Lashed by winds and an icy rain, the First Marine Brigade once again boarded trucks and headed for Pusan. At the end of one full month of operations in South Korea, the marines had contributed mightily toward the successful defense of the Pusan Perimeter.

The cost of their efforts totaled 172 killed and 730 wounded. They had come, and they had conquered. But they were just getting started.

A Rumor of Inchon

On September 13, having completed its withdrawal from the Pusan Perimeter, the First Provisional Marine Brigade disbanded and became part of the First Marine Division. They boarded ship and set sail right away. First rumors held that they were headed for a well-deserved R&R (rest and recuperation) leave in Japan. Later rumors became more factual. Most often mentioned in the rumor mill was the name of Inchon.

CHAPTER THREE

Operation CHROMITE: MacArthur's Greatest Gamble

The birth of General Douglas MacArthur's great notion may never be precisely fixed in time and place. It probably did not spawn as offspring to one intuitive flash; but rather more likely as child to a lifetime of martial reasoning.

At age seventy, MacArthur arguably held firm claim to the title of America's all-time greatest general. Never one to shy from duty, danger, or the potential for enhancing his personal image, he visited the Suwon battlefront on June 29. MacArthur immediately saw the chance to lift himself beyond reach of his nearest rivals for maximum greatness. Out of his immense ego and supreme genius sprang a daring invasion plan.

General Douglas MacArthur was the author of the plan to invade Inchon.

The Plan

The plan still evolving in MacArthur's mind on July 5 was to cut the enemy's line of supply by means of a classic amphibious envelopment introduced high up the Korean coastline near Seoul. This would enable General Walker's Eighth Army to break out of its defensive positions and move northward against a weakening enemy army deprived of supplies. The amphibious force would then cut across the Korean peninsula and serve as an anvil against which Walker's EUSA could hammer the retreating North Koreans.

MacArthur ordered his chief of staff, Major General Edward M. Almond, to begin preparations at once for an amphibious landing at Inchon, code-named Operation CHROMITE.

Shortly after the Wolf-hounds of the 27th Regiment stopped the communist advance at the gates of Taegu, an editorial in the *New York Times* recognized Douglas MacArthur's contribution.

The editorial pointed out that surpassing the welcome news from the battlefront, the principal "cause for satisfaction and assurance surely to be found is the fact that it is Douglas MacArthur who directs this effort in the field. Fate could not have chosen a man better qualified to command the unreserved confidence of the people of this country. Here is a superb strategist and an inspired leader; a man of infinite patience and quiet stability under adverse pressure; a man . . . capable of bold and decisive action. . . .

"In every home in the United States today there must be a sure conviction that if any man can carry out successfully the task which Truman and the Security Council of the United Nations have given him . . . that man is the good soldier in Tokyo who has long since proved to the hilt his ability to serve his country well."

MacArthur quickly paid proper tribute to his soldiers. As July yielded to August, he reported that he believed that "the enemy's plan and great opportunity depended on the speed with which he could overrun South Korea, once he had breached the Han and with overwhelming numbers and with superiors weapons shattered South Korean resistance. This chance he has now lost through the extraordinary speed with which the Eighth Army has been deployed from Japan to stem this rush."

CHROMITE Critics

MacArthur met strong resistance when he tried to raise a force large enough to carry out a landing at Inchon. But at a chance meeting on July 10, 1950, Lieutenant General Lemuel C. Shepherd Jr., commander of Fleet Marine Force Pacific, assured MacArthur that a division of marines could be provided for the operation. MacArthur immediately fired off a request to the Joint Chiefs of Staff in Washington, D.C.: "I understand that a force of division strength can be assembled by the Marines in a matter of six weeks and be in Japan. I hereby make that request at the present time."

MacArthur's wire justified the need for an amphibious envelopment but made no mention of Inchon as a landing site. The Joint Chiefs approved MacArthur's request for marines.

But squabbling among service rivals continued to interfere with CHROMITE preparations. Seeking to eliminate such bickering and gain approval for his plan, MacArthur called for a meeting of high-level officers of all four services. The meeting took place in Tokyo's Dai Ichi Building at 1730 on August 23.

Convinced of the soundness of his strategy, MacArthur compared the thrust of his plan to Wolfe's assault on the French at Quebec in 1759. (British general James Wolfe surprised and defeated French general Louis-Joseph Montcalm during the French and Indian War by scaling the cliffs leading to the Plains of Abraham outside Quebec.) MacArthur did not hesitate to remind those present of the value of surprise in military operations. His dramatic likening of Inchon to Quebec failed to mention that Wolfe was killed during the battle.

Rear Admiral James H. Doyle, slated to assume overall charge of the amphibious operation, later recalled MacArthur's flair for theatrics: "If MacArthur had gone on the stage, you never would have heard of John Barrymore."

MacArthur's stage presence failed to convince everyone of the soundness of his plan. Among his doubters was Lieutenant Commander Arlie Capps. This veteran navy officer later said: "We drew up a list of every conceivable natural and geographic handicap, and Inchon had 'em all."

Critics of MacArthur's plan did not lack for material, for there was much to criticize. An old saying in the Marine Corps states that the conduct and success of any operation "all depends on the terrain and the situation." Operation CHROMITE presented plenty of vexing variables. Natural obstacles headed the list.

"Inchon Is Not Impossible"

Inchon's tides—the second deepest in the world—average a twenty-nine-foot rise and fall, some days rising as high as thirty-six feet. Many channel islands break up the wave action there

and over centuries have caused mud banks to form and extend from shore as far as six thousand yards. Tides run deep enough for oceangoing vessels to clear the mud banks and approach shore on only three days a month. The next dates meeting operational requirements were September 15, October 11, and November 3. MacArthur chose September 15.

Other natural drawbacks included the channel's narrow width and swift current, making ship maneuver difficult. There are few decent landing places. Tides dictated a landing time of 1730. A sunset time of 1842 allowed only an hour and twelve minutes of daylight for troops to land and dig in before an expected enemy counterattack. Plus, as Major General Oliver P. Smith, commander of the First Marine Division, pointed out, Inchon's seawalls were twelve to fifteen feet high and could be easily defended.

Tactically, MacArthur had no way of knowing how many enemy soldiers were defending Inchon. And his plan would land troops in downtown Inchon where every building could be used for defense. Further, no preinvasion bombardment could be brought to bear on the objective else the element of surprise would be lost.

Major General Edward M. Almond and Lieutenant General Lemuel C. Shepherd Jr. confer in Tokyo, Japan, while awaiting the arrival of the Joint Chiefs of Staff. MacArthur hoped to convince the Joint Chiefs of the need to invade Inchon.

Edward M. Almond

General Douglas MacArthur named Major General Edward Mallory Almond to head the newly formed X Corps in September 1950. Almond went on to lead X Corps during the land phase of the Inchon invasion and later acquitted himself well in X Corps's retreat from the Yalu.

Born December 12, 1892, in Luray, Virginia, Almond graduated from Virginia Military Institute in 1915. He was commissioned as a second lieutenant in November 1916. During World War I, he commanded the 12th Machine Gun Battalion, Fourth Infantry Division, in the Aisne-Marne and Meuse-Argonne campaigns. He was wounded in action and received the Silver Star for gallantry.

In World War II, Almond commanded the 92nd Infantry Division—the only "black" division in the U.S. Army to see active combat—during the Italian campaign. His performance as commander of the 92nd Division disappointed black leaders of the day, many of whom considered Almond to be a racist and urged his removal.

Often at the center of controversy, Almond enjoyed something less than respect among many marine officers who served under him. Despite critics of his leadership in Korea, however, it seems fair to say that he got the job done.

Almond retired with the rank of lieutenant general on January 1, 1953. He died on June 11, 1979.

Army chief of staff General J. Lawton Collins opposed the operation, arguing that Inchon is too far from Pusan to yield the desired effect. Also, the First Marine Brigade would have to be restored to the First Marine Division for the landing, thereby weakening General Walker's already hard-pressed forces at Pusan.

Strategically, MacArthur did not know how the Chinese Communists might react. He had already received intelligence reports of Chinese troops moving into Manchuria across the Yalu River from North Korea. Would the Chinese Communists stand by idly while MacArthur landed at Inchon and ultimately destroyed the NKPA? Or would they strike at the Americans while U.S. invasion craft stood jammed together off Inchon and most vulnerable in the narrow Flying Fish Channel? MacArthur could only guess.

A hint of the many reservations held at the time by CHROMITE critics can be found in an unsolicited comment from Admiral Doyle: "General, I have not been asked nor have I volunteered my opinion about this landing. If I were asked, however, the best I can say is that Inchon is not impossible."

Appointment with History

MacArthur remained unswerving in his determination to land at Inchon. He told the Joint Chiefs that his plan would succeed for the very reasons that they foresaw failure, "for the enemy commander will reason that no one would be so brash as to make such an attempt." The only "alternative" to his plan was "a continuation of the savage sacrifice [in the Pusan Perimeter] with no hope of relief in sight." MacArthur made it clear that he would not accept responsibility for such a sacrifice.

"Are you content to let our troops stay in that bloody perimeter like beef cattle in a slaughterhouse?" he asked. "Who will take the responsibility for such a tragedy? Certainly, I will not." Nor was MacArthur willing to wait long for a decision. "I can almost hear the ticking of the second hand of destiny," he warned. "We must act now or we will die."

After another review of his plan, MacArthur continued, "If my estimate [of enemy resistance] is inaccurate, and I should run into a defense with which I cannot cope, I will be there personally and will immediately withdraw our forces before they are committed to a bloody setback. The only loss then will be my professional reputation."

Finally, lowering his voice for maximum dramatic effect, MacArthur concluded, "But Inchon will not fail. Inchon will succeed. And it will save 100,000 lives."

On August 28, the Joint Chiefs, with the concurrence of President Truman, notified MacArthur that Operation CHROMITE had been approved.

But doubts persisted in the minds of the Joint Chiefs and others in Washington. The Chiefs asked MacArthur on September 7 for an updated estimate on the military situation in Korea and a possible reconsideration of his invasion plan. When MacArthur responded in detailed defense of his plan, the Chiefs at last cabled their final approval to him:

WE APPROVE YOUR PLAN AND THE PRESIDENT HAS BEEN SO INFORMED.

Expecting to face fewer than an estimated ten thousand North Korean troops at Inchon, MacArthur's forces numbered approximately seventy thousand by embarkation day. The First Marine Division and the army's Seventh Infantry Division formed the principal components of MacArthur's invasion force. Vice Admiral Dewey Struble, commander of the U.S. Seventh Fleet/Joint Task Force Seven, would direct the amphibious phase of the operation. Major General Edward M. Almond, now commander of the army's X (10th) Corps (while retaining his position as MacArthur's chief of staff), would assume command from Struble once a beachhead had been secured.

Sailors and marines load rafts in preparation for the invasion of Inchon.

On the night of September 12, MacArthur boarded Task Force Seven's command ship *Mount McKinley* at Sasebo, Japan. Amid the violent winds and waters of a raging typhoon, *Mount McKinley* put to sea, carrying the legendary general to his historic Inchon appointment.

CHAPTER FOUR

The Invasion: Situation Well in Hand

General MacArthur's selection of his own chief of staff, Brigadier General Edward M. Almond, to command X Corps displeased the Marine Corps generals who would hold principal roles in carrying out the Inchon invasion. Nor did the navy think highly of MacArthur's choice. Many high-ranking naval officers, veterans of the World War II island campaigns in the Pacific, voiced their doubts about Almond to MacArthur. They pointed out the staff officer's total lack of experience in amphibious operations.

Their concerns fell on deaf ears. MacArthur wanted the command to reside with someone he felt would follow his orders exactly and without question. He remained unyielding in his choice. The invasion got underway as scheduled at 0200, Friday, September 15, 1950.

"Land the Landing Force"

Six- and eight-inch guns from naval vessels anchored out in Flying Fish Channel began a preparatory bombardment of Wolmi-do Island. The heavily fortified island defended the harbor entrance. Its quick capture could mean the difference between the success or failure of the entire operation.

At the first glint of dawn, the barrage of naval gunfire lifted and carrier-based planes struck through towering columns of smoke with continual bombing and strafing attacks. While the aircraft had pounded the island and the causeway tying it to the mainland, navy landing craft filled with U.S. Marines had formed into position and commenced circling in a holding pattern.

Forty-five minutes before daybreak, Rear Admiral James H. Doyle, the attack force commander, ordered signal flags raised on his flagship *Mount McKinley*, their message: "Land the Landing Force."

At the signal, three LSMRs (Landing Ship, Medium, Rocket) surged to within yards of the beach and launched a string of five-inch rocket clusters at the tiny island. The landing craft fanned out into a straight line and started streaking full-throttle toward the shore. When the rocket fire ceased, the LCs (landing crafts) plunged into a veil of smoke and haze and imminent danger.

At 0633, the marines landed on the rocky shore called Green Beach. Thus began what might be called Douglas MacArthur's reenactment of Wolfe's battle on the Plains of Abraham.

Admiral James H. Doyle greets General MacArthur aboard the Mount McKinley *prior to the Inchon invasion. Doyle was to give the signal to land the landing force.*

Green Beach

As had been the case several times during their brief tour in Korea, Lieutenant Colonel Taplett's Third Battalion, Fifth Marines—now part of the First Marine Division—found itself spearheading the attack. Their assignment this time was to secure Wolmi-do. They must first command the high ground called Radio Hill. This they accomplished handily.

With unexpected ease, the marines swept up the slopes almost without opposition. The enemy—although well positioned in protective caves, gun bunkers, and trenches—seemed to lack the stomach for a fight. Less than thirty minutes after hitting the beach, a marine sergeant staked the American flag on the crest of Radio Hill. The entire island fell to the Fifth Marines at 0750, one hour and seventeen minutes after their initial landing.

Taplett then ordered his troopers to move on to the tiny island of Sowolmi-do, tied to Wolmi-do by a 750-yard causeway. When an enemy machine gun cut down on them from the far end of the causeway, Taplett's marines called in air and tank support. Sowolmi-do fell in less than a half-hour.

U.S. troops take four North Koreans prisoner who were hiding in a bunker during the invasion of Wolmi-do Island. The marines took the island easily, in spite of the North Koreans' well-entrenched positions.

General MacArthur watches the shelling of Inchon with field glasses from the Mount McKinley.

General of the Army Douglas MacArthur watched the action through field glasses from offshore on the bridge of the flagship *Mount McKinley.* High-ranking officers surrounded him. Among them were X Corps commander Major General Edward M. Almond, the U.S. Seventh Fleet/Joint Task Force Seven chief Vice Admiral Arthur D. Struble, amphibious force commander Rear Admiral James H. Doyle, First Marine Division commander Major General Oliver P. Smith, and commander of the Pacific Fleet Marine Force Lieutenant General Lemuel C. Shepherd Jr. The commanders shared a common unease.

They all waited anxiously to learn what kind of resistance the enemy would bring to the party. A strong defense here would indicate that the entire Inchon-Seoul area was heavily defended. Taplett's rapid takeover of Wolmi-do and Sowolmi-do did much to relieve their anxiety. MacArthur clapped his hands and laughingly invited the others below decks for a cup of coffee.

Now at ease, MacArthur told Doyle to get a message out to the fleet: "The Navy and the Marine Corps have never shone more brightly than this morning." His praise came well deserved.

In exchange for 17 wounded of their own, Lieutenant Colonel Taplett's troops killed 108 North Korean soldiers and captured 136. Their success prompted Taplett to request permission to continue on and clear the causeway.

Regimental commander Lieutenant Colonel Raymond L. "Ray" Murray denied his request. "No. Stick to the plan," he said.

Taplett tried again: "It's a piece of cake!" He went on to say that he could move tanks right across the causeway, thereby making sure that the rest of the Fifth Marines could land safely at Red Beach. Murray insisted on keeping with the plan. Taplett resigned himself to watching in place and waiting for the plan to unfold.

According to the plan, the First Battalion, Fifth Marines, was to come ashore at Red Beach on the northwest side of Inchon. The First Marine Regiment, as yet untried in Korean combat, would strike Blue Beach on the south side of the city. With the Seventh Marine Regiment in reserve, the Fifth would then push down toward the south, while the First moved up from the south. Together, they would squeeze the life force from the enemy. The army's Seventh Infantry Division, its landing also dictated by the tide swings, would then come ashore and strike toward the east.

At the same time, Walker's Eighth Army was to launch an all-out effort to break out of the Pusan Perimeter. If all went well,

U.S. Marines in landing craft carry ladders that they will use to scale the seawall at Red Beach during the Inchon invasion.

the Seventh Infantry Division would provide the anvil for the Eighth Army's hammer somewhere near Osan, to the southeast.

It should be recalled that Osan was the site of Task Force Smith's defeat at the hands of the NKPA's Fourth Division. The joy of an army victory here would go a long way to erase the agony of their previous loss. Redemption beckoned.

The tide rolled back to its lowest ebb by 1300, stranding Taplett's Third Battalion in a sea of muck. A tense three hours followed, as the marines readied themselves as best they could to ward off a possible enemy counterattack.

While they waited, in the words of Marine Corps historian J. Robert Moskin, "time was the dragon." Perhaps the stranded marines wondered whether even dragons could be worse than waiting.

The tension diminished measurably when a final barrage of naval gunfire commenced at 1430. Their whistling shells, along with bombs and napalm from marine Corsairs and navy Skydivers, set a torch to the entire Inchon waterfront. To close out their bombardment, the navy unleashed no fewer than six thousand rockets, as if to herald the opening of the invasion's second three-hour window of opportunity.

U.S. troops hide in natural trenches along the waterfront of Inchon as they advance.

While They Waited

While Taplett's Third Battalion marines waited on Wolmi-do for the second wave to come ashore at Inchon, the navy started preparing the way at 1430 on September 15. British war correspondent James Cameron wrote:

"The guns began erratically: a few heavy thuds from the cruisers, an occasional bark of five-inch fire, a tuning-up among the harsh orchestra. At what point the playing of the guns merged into the final and awful barrage I do not know; so many things began to take place, a scattered pattern of related happenings gradually coalescing [blending] and building up for the blow.

"All around among the fleet the landing-craft multiplied imperceptibly, took to the water from one could not see exactly where, because the light was failing now—circled and wheeled and marked time and milled about, filling the air with engines. There seemed to be no special hurry. We could not go in until the tide was right; meanwhile we lay offshore in a strange, insolent, businesslike serenity, under whatever guns the North Koreans had, building up the force item by item, squaring the sledge-hammer. The big ships swung gently in the tideway, from time to time coughing heaving gusts of iron towards the town. It began to burn, quite gently at first. What seemed to be a tank or a self-propelled gun sent back some quick, resentful fire, but it soon stopped. Later we found that one ship had thrown a hundred and sixty-five rounds of five-inch ammunition at the one gun. The economics of plenty."

When the din of echoing high explosives faded, a wave of eight LCVPs (Landing Craft, Vehicle, Personnel) formed on a line and turned toward the shore.

Red Beach

At 1733, First Battalion's A Company, led by Captain John R. Stevens, slammed scaling ladders against the seawall along Red Beach. As earlier warriors had once climbed out of trenches to do battle, the marines scrambled out of the boats and up the ladders—and *over the top!*

Life photographer Henry Q. "Hank" Walker recalled, "We went up the ladders, two men at a time. Then we dived over the top of the wall—as we had been told—into a ditch behind the wall."

Luckily, covering fire from the marines on Wolmi-do cleared the seawall and prevented enemy defensive fire.

"A single well-emplaced enemy machine gun," Walker said, "could have chewed the Marines to pieces and badly interfered with the Red Beach landing."

A Company served as the vanguard for the First and Second Battalions of the Fifth Marines. By design, the Fifth Marines were to spread out along a three-thousand-yard arc and direct their attack toward two strategic objectives: the ominous sounding Cemetery Hill on the left, and Observation Hill dead ahead. Once in control of the high ground, they were to fight their way through the city streets, pressing their attack until they reached the tidal basin beyond. The enemy did not intend to make it easy for them. As soon as they cleared the seawall, A Company came under heavy fire from their front and from the north on their left flank. They took several casualties immediately.

The *chigga-chigga-chigga!* of Soviet-made 7.62mm PM (Pulemyot Maxima) machine guns pinned down the First Platoon. Twenty-five-year-old Annapolis graduate First Lieutenant Baldomero Lopez tried to lend a hand with his Third Platoon. The marines continued to take casualties. When Lopez tried to knock out the machine gun with a well-placed grenade, NK fire ripped into his arm and shoulder. He dropped the live grenade and, disabled, found himself unable to pick it up and toss it. Instead, he protected those around him by clawing the grenade under him and absorbing the explosion with his body. He received the Medal of Honor posthumously.

While the First and Third platoons struggled to his right, Second Lieutenant Francis W. Muetzel moved his Second Platoon around to the south of Cemetery Hill and advanced up the street toward a local brewery. At the brewery, he radioed Captain Stevens for further instructions. His company commander ordered him back to Red Beach to help force the NKs out of their positions there. But Muetzel figured he could help more by

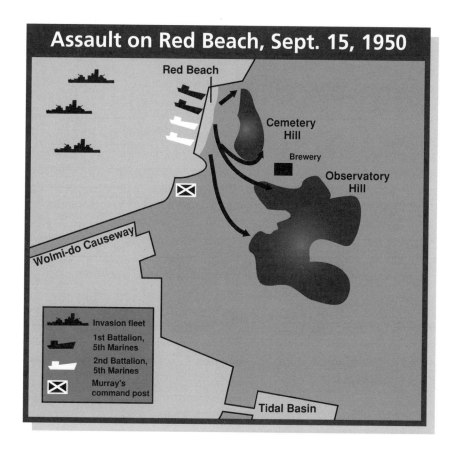

Assault on Red Beach, Sept. 15, 1950

Red Beach

Cemetery Hill

Brewery

Observatory Hill

Wolmi-do Causeway

Invasion fleet

1st Battalion, 5th Marines

2nd Battalion, 5th Marines

Murray's command post

Tidal Basin

taking command of the hill in front of him. So he did. Ten minutes later, the Second Platoon took possession of Cemetery Hill and captured a much surprised enemy mortar crew at its summit. This ended the resistance on Red Beach. Captain Stevens shot off an amber flare to signify victory. A Company paid for the victory with eight dead and twenty-eight wounded.

Arriving at the seawall of Red Beach at 1731, two minutes ahead of A Company, Captain Samuel Jaskilka's E Company marines scaled the four-foot seawall on ladders, hurling grenades over the wall as they climbed. Two platoons moved ashore without casualties. Moving inland rapidly, they together held down a beachhead large enough to allow twenty-two more waves of marines to land. C and D companies were then tasked to secure Observatory Hill, a two-hundred-foot-high mound that stood behind the center of Red Beach.

New York *Herald Tribune* reporter Marguerite "Maggie" Higgins, highly respected for her combat reporting and for her courage during World War II, came ashore in the marines' fifth wave. Automatic weapons fire whizzed and whanged all around her landing craft as it slammed into the seawall. She heard Lieutenant R.J. Shening shout, "Come on, you big, brave Marines!" as he shoved them out of the bow.

A sudden burst of fire too close for a long-life expectancy

prompted her own quick departure. She bailed out over the side into three feet of water, reaching back to snatch up her typewriter before seeking cover behind a nearby mound. After the Fifth Marines secured Red Beach, she retired to the belly of an LST (Landing Ship, Tank) to write the day's story.

She wrote that "a rocket hit a round oil tower and big, ugly smoke rings billowed up." Buildings that lined the docks, she went on, "were brilliant with flames. . . . [I]t looked as though the whole city was burning. . . . The strange sunset, combined with the crimson haze of the flaming docks, was so spectacular that a movie audience would have considered it overdone."

Another story worth writing about involved a marine sergeant on Cemetery Hill: the one who held a live grenade in his hand and thrust it into an NK machine-gun bunker, holding it until it exploded. The sergeant's squad had just been ripped apart by the enemy machine gun.

Not unexpectedly, some confusion resulted when elements of two companies landed on the wrong beaches. This delayed the marine deployment and allowed the North Koreans time to regroup with machine guns on Observatory Hill after the sea and air bombardment lifted.

Eight LSTs loaded with supplies bore down on Red Beach through a hail of NK mortar and machine-gun fire. The navy crews answered with their 20mm and 40mm cannons, spraying both Cemetery and Observatory Hills with uncontrolled fire.

Wounded marines are hoisted aboard Mount McKinley *for treatment.*

Their wild firing drove Lieutenant Muetzel's platoon off the top of Cemetery Hill and into a reverse slope position.

"The Marines ashore were furious and rightly so," Hank Walker remembered. "They turned around and lobbed a few mortar rounds near the LSTs to scare the sailors away from their guns."

As luck would have it, Muetzel's platoon suffered no casualties from friendly fire. But the Second Battalion lost one dead and twenty-three wounded to the navy gunners.

When the LSTs drew close enough to shore, irate marines boarded them and demanded a halt to the indiscriminate shooting.

When the firing halted, the Second Platoon of C Company advanced on Observatory Hill, led by Second Lieutenant Byron L. Magness. A 60mm mortar section followed behind them in support. Mortar man Max Stein managed to still an NK machine gun with grenades along the way, but was wounded in so doing. Magness and his platoon took control of the saddle between the twin crests of Observatory Hill just as daylight faded.

First Battalion commander Newton then radioed Captain Francis I. Fenton Jr. to move B Company off the beach for assault on the northern half of the hill. B Company took six casualties fighting their way up the hill but reached the crest at 2000. Fenton established contact with Magness shortly afterward, and the men dug in for the night.

To the right of Fenton, D Company, commanded by First Lieutenant H.J. Smith, moved up the southern peak of Observatory Hill. They mistakenly believed that Jaskilka's E Company had already secured the peak. But not for long. Second Lieutenant Ray Heck's First Platoon quickly found themselves under withering fire from enemy machine guns to their right. A vicious firefight ensued that lasted fifteen minutes and cost D Company one dead and four wounded. But by midnight, the Americans commanded the southern summit.

With F Company holding down their far right flank, Red Beach belonged to the Fifth Marines.

Blue Beach

In contrast with the fairly well organized and smooth-running operations on Green and Red Beaches, the assault on Blue Beach produced instant chaos. Colonel Lewis B. "Chesty" Puller's First Marines, introduced to combat without benefit of rehearsal or ever having fought together, suffered predictable consequences.

The smoke-filled twilight and wind-lashed rain severely cut their visibility. Unexpectedly strong currents disrupted the orderly waves of landing craft, causing them to scatter and lose direction.

Further confusion grew out of the inexperience of tractor crews, compounded by the lack of compasses and radios. Some of the army's amtracs got stuck in the mud and failed to reach the beach. Others more fortunate managed to drive their marines

An army amtrac carries members of the First Marine Division to Blue Beach. The landing at Blue Beach would be difficult going for the mostly inexperienced marines who landed there.

directly ashore through huge gaps blasted into the seawall earlier by naval gunfire.

The first wave of First Marines hit the beach at 1732.

Lieutenant Colonel Allan Sutter's Second Battalion moved onshore at Blue Beach One in amphibious tractors. They occupied the regiment's left flank without opposition. Unfortunately, the naval shelling had started a landslide that blocked the only road inland. The tractors came to an abrupt halt, unable to surmount the debris.

F Company LVTs fared even less well, bogging down in the mud some three hundred yards offshore. The marines abandoned their mired vehicles and waded in from there. Once ashore, the Second Battalion regrouped and struck out on foot toward the high ground in the northeast. They had work to get done before dark.

Marines of the Third Battalion landed to the right on Blue Beach Two. Sporadic enemy fire greeted them, and G Company's lead LVT also ground to a halt in the offshore muck, temporarily delaying the others. Company commander George C. Westover ordered his men ashore to assume defensive positions on the approaches to the beach. Using aluminum ladders, some of which buckled, and rope cargo nets, the men of G and I companies scaled the fifteen-foot seawall and fanned out along the shoreline.

Once ashore, the two companies moved inland quickly. They came under fire at once from an NK machine gun mounted atop a tower about five-hundred yards inland. Several marines fell victim to it before LVT gunners could knock it out. With the gun out of action, the marines advanced to the outskirts of Inchon. G Company proceeded through the smoke and flames of streets ravaged by artillery and air strikes. I Company swerved off to their right to occupy the tip of Hill 233 at the south end of the beach.

By 0100, the marines had crossed the Inchon-Seoul road about a mile inland. They spent the early hours of September 16 setting up blocking positions across the road.

Back at the beach, the buildup of men and matériel went on all night. Confusion, mishaps, and mistakes continued to plague the First Marines, most of which could be blamed on so little time to prepare properly.

Regimental commander Chesty Puller—a Marine Corps legend and holder of four Navy Crosses—anticipated lots of problems in the early going. Accordingly, he joined his regiment on the beach a half-hour after the initial landing. They needed leadership and that's precisely what they got.

With the help of his officers, many of whom learned their trade during the South Pacific island campaigns, Puller directed the First Marines to a stable position on the division's right flank. Colonel Murray's Fifth Marines stood ashore firmly to his left.

(Left) Marines of the First Division advance quickly inland from Inchon. (Right) LSTs unload men and equipment at Inchon.

Lieutenant General Lemuel Shepherd, Vice Admiral Arthur Struble, General Douglas MacArthur, and Brigadier General Courtney Whitney tour the invasion locations in Inchon Harbor.

Their combined losses for September 15—D-Day—totaled 22 dead, 174 wounded, and 14 nonbattle casualties.

By late evening, their professional conduct under adverse conditions enabled troops of the First and Fifth Marines to claim once again that "the Marine Corps has landed and the situation is well in hand!"

General Douglas MacArthur toured Inchon Harbor in Admiral Struble's barge late that afternoon. Although immensely pleased with the day's accomplishments, he restrained his words in his first cabled report to the Joint Chiefs of Staff in Washington:

> OUR LOSSES ARE LIGHT. . . . THE COMMAND DISTINGUISHED ITSELF. THE WHOLE OPERATION IS PROCEEDING ON SCHEDULE.

In his log entry for September 15, marine commander Major General Oliver P. Smith typically understated the day's activities, concluding that the landings had "gone about as planned."

X Corps commander Brigadier General Edward M. Almond later recalled, "We could already see the landing had been successful the first day, which was really the critical point. Once ashore, we had no fear of being able to take care of any enemy that might meet us eventually."

CHAPTER FIVE

The Advance: Almond Takes Charge

Despite General Almond's confidence about taking care of the enemy, all thirteen thousand marines already ashore on September 16 knew that the real battle still lay ahead. British journalist James Cameron sets the scene:

There was quite a lot of Inchon still standing. One wondered how. There were quite a number of citizens still alive. They came stumbling from the ruins—some of them sound, some of them smashed—numbers of them quite clearly driven into a sort of numbed dementia [madness] by the night of destruction. They ran about, capering crazily or shambling blankly, with a repeated automatic gesture of surrender. Some of them called out as we passed their one English phrase, as a kind of password: "Sank you! Sank you!" and the irony of that [changed] the [odd -looking] into the [horrible].

Aboard *Mount McKinley*, General MacArthur approached General Oliver P. Smith as he was preparing to debark and establish the First Marine Division command post ashore. "Good luck, General Smith," MacArthur said. "Take Kimpo Airfield as soon as you can."

Tank Destroyers

On orders from General Smith, Colonel Murray's Fifth Marines marched through the southern sector of Inchon. They made no attempt to clear enemy troops from the city, content to leave the slow, bloody "mopping up" chores to the able and eager troops of the first ROK Marine Regiment. Three months earlier, North Korean soldiers had shown no mercy to ROK supporters. The ROK Marines looked forward to avenging communist cruelties. The streets of Inchon would soon run red with the blood of both sides.

At 0730, the Fifth Marines linked up with Puller's First Marines about three miles inland, Puller's position from the night before. The invasion's success was assured.

Three miles east of Inchon, an early flight of eight marine Corsairs off the carrier *Sicily* spotted six Soviet-made T-34 tanks on the Inchon-Seoul road. The unescorted tanks were heading toward Inchon. The Corsairs, led by Major Robert Floeck of Marine Fighter Squadron 214, attacked the T-34s immediately with napalm and 500-pound bombs. They destroyed three of the six enemy tanks. Marine M-26 Pershing tanks eliminated the other three T-34s.

Captain William F. Simpson's Corsair took a hit from North Korean machine-gun fire that blew out the plane's oil system. The aircraft failed to respond when Simpson tried to pull out of his attack dive. It disappeared upon impact in a mighty explosion.

(Left) Korean civilians in Inchon flee the ruined and burning city. (Right) A lone child cries out for help amid the ruins of Inchon.

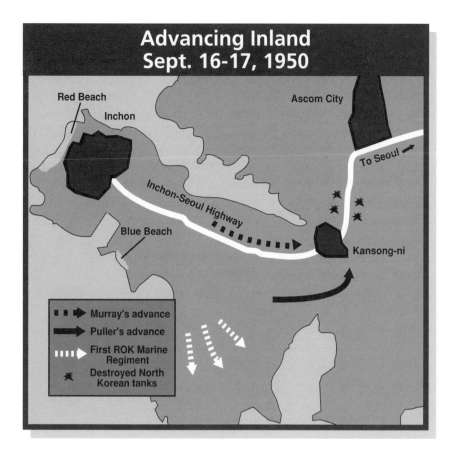

Advancing Inland
Sept. 16-17, 1950

Red Beach

Inchon

Ascom City

To Seoul →

Inchon-Seoul Highway

Blue Beach

Kansong-ni

■ ■ ➡ Murray's advance
➡ Puller's advance
❚❚❚❚ First ROK Marine Regiment
✴ Destroyed North Korean tanks

The First and Fifth Regiments then moved east together along the Inchon-Seoul road. They reached a point about five miles inland by the end of the day and dug in for the night.

In the darkness before dawn on September 17, six more North Korean T-34s moved west on the Inchon-Seoul road with an infantry escort. This time, a bazooka team from Murray's First Marines knocked out one T-34. Fire from marine M-26s and 75mm recoilless rifles set the other five aflame. Puller's First Marines joined the attack from the right side of the road and helped to wipe out two hundred North Korean infantry troops. One marine rifleman was slightly wounded.

MacArthur Tours the Front

General MacArthur came ashore shortly after dawn that morning to tour the battlefront and enjoy the bittersweet fruit of his victory. Viewing the shattered NKPA positions and corpses at dockside seemed to please him greatly.

Joking with his personal physician, MacArthur pointed to one of the dead North Koreans and said, "There's a patient you'll never have to work on." MacArthur then boarded a jeep and headed inland, along with a caravan of high-ranking officers, reporters, and photographers to view the action.

General MacArthur often recklessly disregarded his own safety to tour recent battlefields. In Korea, he used such tours as media events.

MacArthur's "tour" afforded him another fine opportunity to appear before the media as some kind of modern-day Alexander. And he loved every minute of it. Much to the dismay of battlefield commanders responsible for his safety, MacArthur often displayed a reckless disregard for personal danger. He was cocky, vain, and foolhardy, perhaps, but he was no coward.

The caravan motored east along the Inchon-Seoul road toward Chesty Puller's First Marines. MacArthur had decided to award the Silver Star to Puller. (No one seemed to know just what Puller had done lately to deserve the medal, not even Puller. MacArthur was perhaps influenced by sentiment, as he had long admired the plucky marine's incredible heroism during the Second World War.) A message radioed ahead from the jeep caravan summoning Puller to a meeting with MacArthur found Puller busy attacking an enemy-held ridge. Puller snapped brief instructions to his radio operator: "Signal them that we're fighting our way for every foot of ground. I can't leave here. If he wants to decorate, he'll have to come up here."

Puller's sassiness seemed to delight MacArthur. He informed his comrades to get back in their jeeps. They would visit Puller.

When the jeep caravan neared the top of Puller's steep ridge, MacArthur's jeep stalled out. His party got out and walked the rest of the way, the sound of small-arms fire crackling in the distance. Puller and MacArthur exchanged snappy salutes. After all that fuss, MacArthur dug around in his pockets for a Silver Star and could not find one.

Colonel Lewis B. Puller, General Douglas MacArthur, Major General Oliver P. Smith, and Vice Admiral Arthur Struble observe a marine regiment in action on a hill in Korea. MacArthur took pleasure in such tours.

"Make a note of that," he told reporters with the party. The general would have to send the medal along later. Oh, well.

Back down on the road, the caravan continued on until it came upon the site where marine Corsairs had destroyed the T-34s the day before. MacArthur dismounted and examined the charred remnants of the North Korean tanks.

"Considering that they're Russian," he said, "these tanks are in the condition I desire them to be.'

Then Lieutenant Colonel Raymond Murray, commander of the First Marines, volunteered that "these are yesterday's kills. If you want to see some fresh-killed tanks, we have some just up the road." He was referring to the six tanks destroyed by his First Marines that morning.

Major General Oliver P. Smith, First Marine Division commander and member of the jeep party, cringed. Small-arms fire still echoed through the hills. The last thing he wanted was to see his commander in chief killed—especially in a marine sector.

Marines in the Right Spot

Continuing on down the road, MacArthur's caravan was soon halted by a young marine officer waving his arms.

"General, you can't come up here!" he said.

MacArthur smiled at him and asked, "And why not?"

"We've just knocked out six Red [North Korean] tanks over the top of this hill," the young officer answered.

"That was the proper thing to do," MacArthur said, and the caravan rolled on.

In due course, the jeeps arrived at the scene of the recent tank battle. Six North Korean T-34s sat still burning, surrounded by scores of bodies.

Lieutenant General Lemuel C. Shepherd Jr., Fleet Marine Force commander, another member of MacArthur's party, recalled that some of the bodies lay "half-cooked on top of several of the tanks."

MacArthur prodded one dead enemy body with his toe. "That's the way I like to see them!" he said. "A good sight for my old eyes!" MacArthur viewed the smoking tanks in silence, striking some battlefield poses to oblige the photographers. Finally, MacArthur turned to General Shepherd and Joint Task Force Seven chief Vice Admiral Arthur D. Struble. "Well done," he said.

By then, X Corps commander Major General Edward M. Almond had heard about enough praise for the Marine Corps. He expressed himself to General Shepherd in poorly pretended good humor.

"You damned Marines! You always seem to be in the right spot at the right time. Hell, we've been fighting this battle with army troops [prior to the Inchon invasion] but MacArthur would arrive just as the Marines had knocked out six enemy tanks."

Shepherd smiled without comment.

"A Good Man Under Fire"

Marguerite "Maggie" Higgins, premier foreign correspondent for the New York *Herald Tribune*, shared the life of American GIs in Korea. Exposing herself to the daily hardships and dangers of front-line news gathering became routine to the first woman to win a Pulitzer Prize for international reporting.

Maggie became a familiar sight wherever the action was, because that's where the stories were. Often she would type out her stories on the hood of a jeep, then sleep on the ground with whatever unit she was covering.

"Maggie's the only gal you can brag about sleeping with and not be a cad," one soldier commented.

Even the rival *New York Times* acknowledged after the war that "Marguerite Higgins got stories other reporters didn't get."

After Inchon, Maggie accompanied the Fifth Marines in their long march south from the Chosin Reservoir. Then, emotionally spent, and suffering from bronchitis, acute sinusitis, recurrent malaria, dysentery, and jaundice, she returned to the States where she entered a hospital for treatment.

Maggie recovered well and went on to cover other stories and battles. But it is for her grit and reporting during the Korean War—*her* war—that Marguerite Higgins will always be remembered.

Keyes Beech of the *Chicago Daily News*, her colleague and friend in Korea, perhaps best described her. "She was a good man under fire," he said.

Personality Conflict

Although General MacArthur did not set a hard and fast date for liberating Seoul, he wanted it done quickly. The sooner the better, he figured, to maximize both military advantage and negative effects on enemy morale. He suggested to General Almond that the South Korean capital probably could be set free within "five days" of the landing—or by September 20.

Almond doubted that his forces could wrap up the operation within five days. But he guaranteed MacArthur that Seoul would be liberated within ten days, which meant by September 25. MacArthur concurred. Almond then informed marine commander General Oliver Smith that MacArthur wanted Seoul taken by September 25 "exactly three months after the date that the North Koreans invaded South Korea." Almond also indicated to Smith that MacArthur expected a communiqué to that effect. The marines were expected to adhere to that schedule. Almond intended to see that they did.

General Smith called the UN advance on Seoul "one of those routine operations that read easier in the newspapers than on the ground." Smith did not intend to subject his troops to a schedule

Major General Oliver P. Smith talks with Major General Edward M. Almond. Almond was eager to adhere to MacArthur's schedule for winning the war in Korea while Smith considered the schedule another one of MacArthur's publicity stunts.

dictated by public relations. "I told [Almond] that I couldn't guarantee anything; that was up to the enemy. We'd do the best we could and go as fast as we could."

But Almond became obsessed with keeping his September 25 commitment with General MacArthur. Almond later assessed Smith as being "overly cautious" in carrying out orders. He added that Smith "always had excuses for not performing at the required time the task he was requested to do."

According to Almond's G-3 (operations officer), Colonel John H. "Jack" Chiles, "The Marines were exasperatingly deliberate at a time when rapid maneuver was imperative." He remembered Almond and Smith as being outwardly cordial while growing to "hate each other." Chiles sensed that "Smith resented being under an Army commander of any sort" and "came as close to getting insubordinate as he could be."

In fairness, Chiles remembered Almond as being "very proud, very intolerant," and "also overbearing." Almond continually went around Smith on the battlefield, often issuing orders directly to Colonels Murray and Puller. Without a helicopter of his own, Almond thought nothing of snatching Smith's to convey his orders.

From Smith's viewpoint, as he wrote later, he had "little confidence" in the "tactical judgment" of X Corps (another way of saying Almond) or in the "realism of its [his] planning."

Colonel Alpha L. Bowser, Smith's operations officer, thought that army generals "were still suffering from the phase of the grand sweeps of the broad arrow operations of Europe." The army "failed to appreciate the fact that an Oriental who is bypassed is not out of the ball game. He is not a German or an Italian, and he doesn't get out on the road and hold up his hand. He gets in a hole with a sack full of rice and a few rounds of ammunition and he'll kill anyone that he has a chance to kill."

Bowser recalled that the marines and the army exchanged " a great deal of unkind words" regarding North Korean guerrilla activities to the rear and on both flanks.

Chiles summed up the relationship between Almond and Smith: "It was a very unfortunate personality conflict." The same might be said of the relationship between the U.S. Army and the Marine Corps.

Marines Advance

After MacArthur's visit to the front, Murray's Fifth Marines pushed on. East of Ascom City, just east of Inchon, the marines swerved north and, along with the Korean Marines Third Battalion, advanced on Kimpo airfield. Kimpo, with its six-thousand-foot concrete runway, is South Korea's largest air base. MacArthur wanted it taken quickly so that his Fifth Air Force—then flying from bases in Japan—could operate more efficiently.

Murray's marines obliged. The Fifth Marines commenced an assault on the airfield in the late afternoon of September 17, eliminating the last enemy resistance by 0500 the next morning.

Meanwhile, Puller's First Marines were meeting strong enemy resistance from elements of the 18th NKPA Division commanding the hills along the approach to Yongdungpo. Yongdungpo, a run-down industrial suburb, lies across the Han River, slightly southwest of Seoul. The North Koreans counterattacked the marines outside Sosa, located midway between Ascom City and Yongdungpo, late on September 17. Pushed back and stalled temporarily, the First Marines regained the lost ground the next day and continued their drive toward Yongdungpo.

Along the way, the marines captured a group of North Korean stragglers hiding in a cave. Two marines were assigned to escort the captives to the rear, but the escorts returned almost at once. In explanation of their speedy return, they said, "Prisoners are too much of a bother right now."

Sharing the Credit

General Almond had by then grown alarmed that the marines might receive too much credit for American successes to date in the Korean fighting. He was eager to involve the army in whatever

ROK Marines move toward the Han River from Kimpo airfield to defend against the North Korean forces.

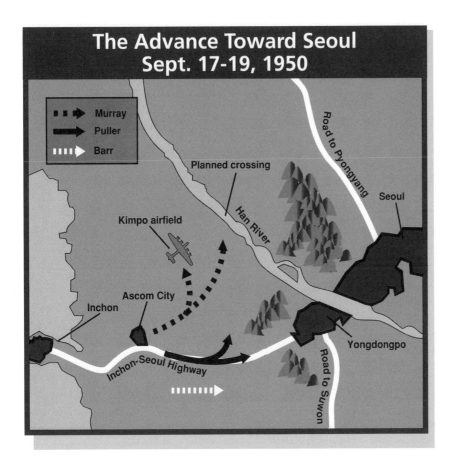

The Advance Toward Seoul
Sept. 17-19, 1950

- ▪▪▶ Murray
- ▬▬▶ Puller
- ▯▯▶ Barr

Planned crossing

Road to Pyongyang

Seoul

Han River

Kimpo airfield

Ascom City

Inchon

Yongdongpo

Road to Suwon

Inchon-Seoul Highway

glory there was yet to be claimed. With that in mind, Almond off-loaded the 32nd Infantry Regiment of Major General David G. Barr's Seventh Infantry Division in Inchon on September 18 and rushed the soldiers into action. The rest of the division was to follow as soon as possible.

Next to Almond, Barr was the senior army general in the Inchon sector. Opinions as to Barr's capabilities varied.

One of Almond's staff officers wrote, "He [Barr] was an inept, vacillating commander who exasperated General Almond continuously . . . only their long friendship kept him from being relieved by General Almond."

Another X Corps staffer said, "He was a fine man but he didn't have a clue as to how a division worked."

In Barr's behalf, Seventh Division intelligence officer John W. "Bill" Paddock wrote, "Barr was a hellova [sic] better division commander than Almond was a corps commander."

Such is the stuff of service rivalries: a soldier's worth depends on the point of view. In this instance, Barr failed to maintain communications with the First Marines. The marines did not have a hint as to where Barr's troops were or what they were doing. Puller's marines immediately lost all confidence in Barr and his soldiers. But all ended well.

"Right Up the Middle"

More than a few army officers expressed dismay at some of the hell-bent-for-leather tactics used by the marines in Korea and throughout their history.

Lieutenant Colonel John "Iron Mike" Michaelis, commander of the 27th Infantry Regiment's Wolfhounds, noted critically that "the Marines were always too keen on frontal attacks."

X Corps' operations officer, Lieutenant Colonel Ellis Williamson, said, "The Marines are a product of their history. They are trained, indoctrinated, to go from ship to shore, then to keep running forward until they have taken the pressure off the beachhead. The thought of outflanking a position would horrify a man like 'Chesty' Puller. We used to call the Marines 'the nursery rhyme soldiers' because their motto was: 'Hey diddle diddle, right up the middle.' On that march to Seoul, I saw Marines doing things no army outfit would think of. I watched them crossing the great sweep of wide open ground in front of Kimpo airfield, hundreds of young men rising up and starting across the flats in open order. They took far more casualties than we considered appropriate."

While a fire rages in a building across the square, weary, battle-seasoned marines pause for a smoke amid the wreckage of a fire-gutted Korean city before resuming their search for North Korean troops.

Barr's 32nd Infantry Regiment moved swiftly eastward and secured the right flank of the First Marines. Troops of the 32nd Regiment's First Battalion seized the high ground at Anyang, south of Yongdungpo, on September 21. This cut the railroad line and the road from Suwon, both of which were used to reinforce the NKPA.

Barr's soldiers then branched off southward on the Seoul-Suwon road toward the airstrip at Suwon, about twenty-one miles south of Seoul. They experienced some initial difficulty finding the airstrip on the night of September 21 but found it the next morning. After prevailing in a tank skirmish and overcoming some stubborn NK infantry resistance, troops of the 32nd Infantry took control of the airfield on September 22.

Later that day, elements of the 31st Infantry Regiment took over occupation of the Suwon airfield. Additional elements of Barr's Seventh Division continued on south to establish a roadblock in the area of nearby Osan (where Task Force Smith had originally engaged the enemy). Part of their mission was to cut off the flow of NK reinforcements heading toward Seoul. Beyond that, they were to hold in place to await the breakout of Walker's Eighth Army, some 160 miles to the south.

They were soon to become the "anvil" for Walker's "hammer," thereby allaying Almond's fears that the marines would get credit for more than their share of glory.

Closing In on Seoul

Murray's Fifth Marines pressed on across Kimpo airfield, reaching the south bank of the Han River bordering Seoul by close of day on September 18. They occupied the high ground north of Yongdungpo—hills 80, 85, and 118—until late the following day but the First Battalion, Fifth Marines, pulled off hills 80 and 85 that evening to prepare for crossing the Han. They left the hills temporarily unoccupied. Marines from Puller's First Battalion were scheduled to take over the positions before dark.

Unfortunately for the marines, Puller's First Battalion was delayed when the road became too poor for truck traffic. Forced to cover the remaining eleven miles on foot, Puller's men arrived at Hill 118 after dark. Rather than move into hostile territory in the dark, the marines decided to wait until daylight to reoccupy hills 80 and 85. That night, North Korean troops slipped back onto the hills, forcing the marines to counterattack the next morning to recapture the hills. The First Marines took back the two hills the next day in a furious hand-to-hand engagement. But only at the cost of many more marine lives.

Reporters tour a hangar destroyed by U.S. troops at Kimpo airfield.

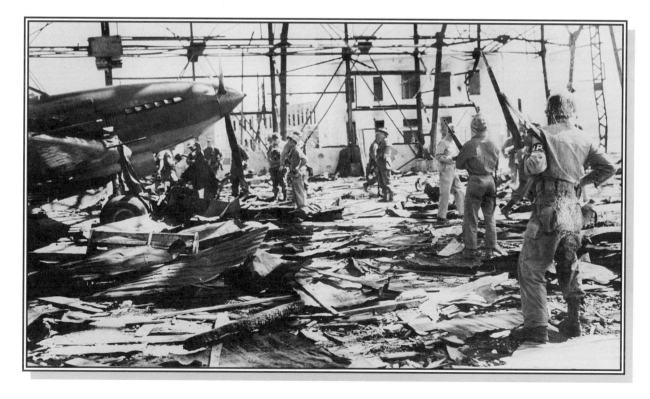

Shoot-Out at Yongdungpo

Ed Simmons, then a marine major and commander of a weapons company, recalled:

At Yongdungpo we had our first really hard fight. The town is on the opposite bank of the Han River from Seoul, roughly the same position that Brooklyn occupies relative to New York City, and we had a very tough fight there.

All three battalions of our regiment were involved in it. My own weapons company was on the high ground overlooking the town, supposedly in reserve, but everyone was called into the fight, and we came down off the high ground and crossed some dried overgrown rice paddies to a canal. The First Battalion came across those rice paddies at an angle to us, and watching them come was like watching a scene from World War One, the companies moving forward in a long line through waist-high grass, with shot and shell going off all around them.

We had a hard time getting across the canal. We were up against this dike, and again it was like World War One, one rifle platoon after another going over the top, right into the teeth of heavy machine-gun fire from the other side. A lot of men were hit. . . . Well, we had to reduce the machine-gun fire that was tearing us up. So I brought up my own heavy machine guns and had the crews set them up on the brow of the dike. And we had a shoot-out. Water-cooled Brownings on Our side, water-cooled Maxims [7.62 mm Pulyemot Maximas] on the other, blasting away at each other across this narrow canal.

They quit first. The North Koreans pulled back out of their positions, and we crossed the canal.

On September 20, the North Koreans turned back the Fifth Marines as they attempted to cross the Han. Murray's marines tried crossing the river again the next day, this time with success. Colonel Homer L. Litzenberg's Seventh Marine Regiment had debarked at Inchon three days earlier and was moving into support positions west of Seoul. At the same time, Puller's First Marines assaulted Yongdungpo. The city fell on the night of September 21.

With the beachhead firmly established and the battle for Seoul set to begin, the navy's Seventh Task Force handed over command responsibility for Operation CHROMITE to X Corps. General Almond took charge.

CHAPTER SIX

The Breakout: North from Naktong

An Eighth United States Army (EUSA) battle plan issued at the time of the Inchon landing stated: "Currently the enemy is on the offensive and retains this capability in all general sectors of the Perimeter. It is not expected that this capability will decline in the immediate future."

American intelligence estimated North Korean strength around the Naktong (Pusan) Perimeter at 101,147. But it was later determined that the NKPA comprised only 70,000 surviving troops on September 16. And of the 70,000, only about 21,000 were hardened combat veterans. The rest consisted of ill-trained replacements. While American and ROK forces by then totaled about 150,000, some South Korean elements lacked leadership and training and were less than effective. Although Walker did not know it at the time, his forces held a clear advantage over a weakening enemy.

Such was the situation when the United States Eighth Army commenced its breakout from the Naktong Perimeter at precisely 0900 on September 16, 1950.

Walker's Plan

General Walker's plan called for a three-pronged attack:

(1) In the Taegu (Naktong Bulge and northwest) sector, the 24th Infantry and the First Cavalry Divisions, now combined to form I (Eye) Corps, would cross the Naktong River near Waegwan and strike northwest up the road toward Taejon and beyond. The 24th would spearhead the attack, with the

First Cavalry behind. Advance units of the 24th Division should then link up with X Corps at Suwon.

(2) The Second and 25th Infantry Divisions, joined now as IX (Ninth) Corps, would advance out of the southwest sector and slash northwest across the peninsula along three mostly parallel roads toward Kunsan.

(3) Out of the northeast sector, the six available ROK divisions would strike north into the Taebaek Mountains and continue up the east coast road.

Walker's breakout did not proceed as planned. Heavy rains and dense fog canceled U.S. air support. And the North Koreans chose the same day to launch an offensive of their own.

MacArthur's master strategy had anticipated that the North Koreans, upon learning that they were cut off by his flanking movement at Inchon, would beat a hasty retreat. But the North Korean commanders neglected to inform their troops of MacArthur's move to the north. They figured quite correctly that their troops would fight better without benefit of such knowledge.

Troops fire on the enemy along the Naktong River north of Taegu.

Soldiers throw grenades and lay down artillery fire in hopes of taking Hill 300 from the North Koreans.

The NKPA's renewed initiative and firm resistance resulted in four major breakout battles. Heavy fighting erupted around the perimeter in the southwest sector, the Naktong Bulge, and the northwest and northeast sectors.

Breakout Bogs Down

In IX Corps's southwest sector, the 25th Infantry Division tried to honor Walker's timetable on September 16 but ran smack into the determined remnants of the NKPA Sixth and Seventh Divisions. Hampered by rough terrain, poor weather, and lack of air support, the U.S. troops were unable to dislodge the NK soldiers from their mountain strongholds. The 25th Division's offensive stalled immediately and remained stalled until September 19. Then, strangely, the North Koreans abandoned their lofty positions on their own. Whether they left under orders or just broke and ran is not known.

The 25th Infantry Division then began a slow, cautious advance toward the much-fought-over town of Chinju. Their efforts hardly represented the lightning-like breakthrough that Walker had envisioned, but it was a start.

North of the 25th Division, the Second Infantry Division also jumped off on September 16, with a little more success than their IX Corps comrades. Elements of the Second Division captured Hill 208, on the Naktong's east bank overlooking the river. Two of the division's companies crossed the Naktong against a twelve-foot-deep current on September 18.

By September 19, the Second Division had cleared NKPA forces from the Naktong's east bank. Two more battalions crossed the Naktong. Engineers spanned the river with a pontoon bridge in preparation for a major crossing. Poor weather and no air support also hampered the Second Division, as did a shortage of ammunition. Colonel Paul L. Freeman Jr., commander of the 23rd Infantry Regiment, recalled:

> In Korea we were always conserving ammunition. We were always on the brink of running out. Always scared to death that we were going to get caught with no ammunition. I believe it was rationed the whole time I was there. Even small-arms ammunition . . . we never had enough.

The NKPA Fourth and Ninth Divisions still held the high ground on the Naktong's west bank. To the west of them stood the NKPA 10th Division, which until then had done nothing. The Americans believed that the North Koreans were regrouping for a strong counterattack. The Second Division still had work to do.

In I Corps's northwest sector, the Fifth Regimental Combat Team and elements of the First Cavalry Division advanced painfully slowly against the NKPA Third Division during September 16-18. The Third Battalion, Fifth Cavalry Regiment, attacked Hill 174 eleven times before finally securing it. The hill had changed possession seven times prior to that. North Korean bodies lay scattered about the shell-scarred hillside, some fresh and some not. Victor Fox, an L Company soldier, well remembered Hill 174:

> Around our positions the enemy dead lay in terrible positions. . . . Most had been badly mangled by artillery fire . . . [and] the stench . . . became stifling. . . . In all the time I spent on Hill 174 there was never time to remove the corpses that surrounded us. The continual, deadly firefight made such a venture an impossibility.

To the south of the Fifth RCT, engineers failed to ford the Kumho River on time, thus delaying the 24th Division's attempt to cross the Naktong River to the west. The delay caused units of the 24th Division to get badly shot up during a daylight crossing

(Left) Typical of the fighting at the Naktong Perimeter, these men advance in the hopes of securing this hill from the North Koreans. (Right) M-26 tanks cross over the Naktong River using an underwater crossing consisting of rocks and sandbags to reinforce the riverbed.

on September 19. At the same time, the Eighth Cavalry regiment tried unsuccessfully to clear the Bowling Alley area of NKPA First and 13th Division remnants.

September 19 found the Fifth RCT and Fifth Cavalry Regiment unable to advance on Waegwan. The 21st Infantry Regiment had crossed the Naktong but was under heavy enemy attack and in danger of becoming cut off or forced to retreat. And the Eighth Cavalry Regiment, reinforced by the Seventh Cavalry Regiment, was stuck in place in the Bowling Alley.

Clearly, the breakout was bogged down.

A Break in the Weather

When the foul weather lifted on September 19, U.S. airplanes took to the sky. Along with napalm and high explosives, the bombers dropped thousands of leaflets that featured a map showing the amphibious landing at Inchon and the following message:

UNITED NATIONS FORCES HAVE LANDED AT INCHON

Officers and men of North Korea, powerful UN forces have landed at Inchon and are advancing rapidly. You can see from this map how hopeless your situation has become. Your supply lines cannot reach you, nor can you withdraw to the north. The odds against you are tremendous. Fifty-three out of the 59 countries in the UN are opposing you. You are outnumbered in equipment, manpower and firepower. Surrender or die. Come over to the UN side and you will get food and prompt medical care.

Following this encouragement, the North Koreans started to lose their taste for battle. And if they did not like the snacks UN forces had served so far, they would surely not like the main courses soon to follow.

Like Bubbles in the Wind

On September 19, the Third NKPA Division suddenly abandoned its hilltop positions at Waegwan and fled west across the Naktong River. The Fifth RCT entered the town late that afternoon and cleared it of NK stragglers the next day.

Also on September 19, the ROK First Division advanced thirteen miles into mountains north of Taegu in the northeast sector and took up positions behind the First and 13th NKPA Divisions. Afraid that its avenue of retreat might be severed, the First NKPA Division pulled out right away.

The next day, the ROK Third Division captured Pohang on the east coast and forced the Fifth NKPA Division to commence a rapid withdrawal northward. The ROK troops then started making sweeping advances in the mountains bordering the east coast.

The U.S. First Cavalry Division fought through stubborn North Korean defenders in the Bowling Alley battlefield area and finally recaptured Tabu on September 21.

September 22 saw the Second Infantry Division continuing to encounter strong NKPA resistance west of the Naktong. One of the war's great tragedies also occurred on that day.

Soldiers of the Scottish Argyll Battalion of the British 27th Brigade occupied Hill 272 while in pursuit of the Tenth NKPA Division near Songju. Under attack by NK troops from nearby Hill 388, the Argylls called for a U.S. air strike on Hill 388. Soon three U.S. F-51 Mustang fighter-bombers arrived on scene. Sadly, the American pilots confused the hills and attacked the Argylls with napalm and bombs, inflicting sixty British casualties.

By September 23, the North Koreans had withdrawn northward in full flight, with UN forces pursuing rapidly along almost every road and highway heading toward the border. Some North Korean soldiers formed blocking parties and fought like tigers to enable their comrades to escape. Blown bridges and antitank mines slowed the American advance only briefly.

While some NK soldiers fought to the end, others stood by idly and waited to surrender. Soon the once-proud divisions of General Choe Yong-gun scattered and disappeared like soap bubbles in the autumn wind.

North Korean prisoners are guarded by South Korean marines before their removal to a POW camp.

Task Force Lynch

To spearhead the Eighth Army's drive northward to join forces with Almond's X Corps, First Cavalry Division commander Major General Hobart R. Gay formed Task Force Lynch. The TF was made up of the Third Battalion of the Seventh Cavalry Regiment, reinforced by an engineer company, seven M4A3 medium tanks from another battalion, a reconnaissance platoon, a tactical air party, and heavy mortar and artillery support units. Like most task forces, this unit was named for its leader.

Lieutenant Colonel James H. Lynch launched his northward drive from the Bowling Alley–Tabu battleground north of Taegu at 0800 on September 22. TF Lynch reached the town of Naktong that night at 2230. Lynch sent two infantry companies across the Naktong River at 0430 the next morning to secure the west bank.

In the meantime, Lynch's engineers improved Naktong's underwater bridge. Before noon on September 24, Lynch's tanks had crossed the river safely. The TF then proceeded to Poun, about thirty miles up the road, where it regrouped the next day. At 1130 on September 26, Task Force Lynch rolled out of Poun. The spectacular American advance that followed reminded observers of General George S. Patton's Third Army racing across Europe in 1944.

With Lieutenant Robert W. Baker's six-tank platoon leading the way, the miles slipped by without incident. "We went for many miles without opposition," Colonel Lynch wrote, "and with cheering crowds of South Koreans greeting us along the way."

At Chongju, sixty-four miles north of Poun, the tanks ran out of gas about 1800. Unexpectedly, three North Korean trucks ran into Lynch's reconnaissance jeep. The NKs fled on foot. The Americans found enough gas in cans in the trucks to refuel Baker's tanks. By 2000, the task force was rolling northwest again.

Lynch then ordered all his vehicles to use their lights. "The moon had risen but a cloudy night obscured vision," he wrote. "Behind me were miles of vehicle lights winding their way through enemy-held territory—a weird sight to behold."

Turning north, the TF began meeting North Korean troops. Lynch "shot up one truckload" but passed by most.

About 2030, Baker's tanks reached Chonan, which was still occupied by North Korean soldiers. Baker pulled up at a guard post and popped his head out of the lead tank.

"Osan?" Baker asked, pointing down one of the town's streets. The guard nodded yes. When it dawned on the guard that Baker was an American, he fled his post in a hurry. Other North Koreans stood around and calmly watched the Americans pass through unopposed.

Three miles south of Osan, Baker's tanks—then out of touch with the rest of the task force—took and returned enemy fire. An

"A Bunch of Nervous Nellies"

Few members of the U.S. military establishment anticipated the great success of the Inchon landing and subsequent breakout from the Naktong (Pusan) Perimeter. The doubters included General Omar N. Bradley, the first chairman of the Joint Chiefs of Staff. Bradley later wrote:

Inchon proved to be the luckiest military operation in history.

Walker's Eight Army had been instructed to attack out of the Pusan perimeter on D plus 1, September 16. However, the North Koreans were apparently slow to grasp the fact that they were trapped, and they fiercely resisted Walker's attack. For a full week the North Korean Army held. Then, on September 22, it buckled and Walker broke out at full speed. With little or no concern for his flanks, he ordered his men to race north and west and destroy the routed enemy.

On September 26, units of the 1st Cavalry and the 7th Division linked up near Osan. Seoul fell to the Marines on September 26

and 27. Meanwhile, the I ROK Corps dashed up the east coast of Korea virtually unopposed. The decimated North Korean Army fled north, helter-skelter.

The swiftness and magnitude of the victory was mind-boggling. . . . MacArthur was deservedly canonized [glorified] as a "military genius." Inchon was his boldest and most dazzling victory. In hindsight, the JCS [Joint Chiefs of Staff] seemed like a bunch of nervous Nellies to have doubted.

General Omar Bradley was amazed that MacArthur's daring plan had worked so successfully and easily.

NK antitank shell sheared off a machine-gun mount from Baker's third tank and killed one American.

Baker's tanks started receiving more fire north of Osan. This time it was friendly fire. Luckily, an exploding phosphorus shell revealed the white star on one of Baker's tanks and an all-American shoot-out was averted.

Baker's half-dozen tanks had arrived intact. Task Force Lynch had amazingly covered 106 miles in one day, establishing contact with elements of General Barr's Seventh Infantry Division near Osan at 2226 on September 26.

The Eighth Army's breakout and drive north from Naktong was completed when EUSA and X Corps linked up at 0826 the next day.

CHAPTER SEVEN

The Liberation: "Well and Nobly Done"

The battle for Seoul—the end prize in MacArthur's master plan—began early on September 22. Positioned around the city's western periphery were about twenty thousand troops belonging to the 25th NKPA Brigade and the 78th NKPA Independent regiment. Commanded by Major General Wol Ki Chan, the determined defenders occupied the high ground surrounding the city. Their positions were firmly entrenched and heavily protected with interlocking fields of fire. The Han River formed an additional natural barrier, splitting Major General Oliver P. Smith's First Marine Division and making it more difficult for Smith to coordinate his attack. Inside the city, every steel-reinforced concrete building stood as an armed fortress in the path of Smith's attacking marines.

But of the problems facing Smith, perhaps X Corps commander Major General Edward M. Almond loomed largest of all. Almond told Smith that he was "in a hurry" to cross the Han River. To please General MacArthur, Almond kept constant pressure on the marines to capture Seoul by September 25. MacArthur wanted to announce Seoul's liberation to the world three months to the day after the North Koreans had invaded South Korea.

Smith objected to a timetable based on enhancing MacArthur's image rather than on military necessity. MacArthur's image was not worth the life of one marine. Moreover, Smith bitterly resented what he considered undue interference from a superior whom he felt to be unqualified and inept.

Smith's operations officer, Colonel Alpha Bowser, noted that Almond "had a habit of treating the Han River like it had five or six bridges intact across it, and of course it had none."

Major General Smith resented Major General Almond's ineptitude and insistence on adhering to MacArthur's schedule.

Two of Smith's three regiments had yet to cross the river. Relations between the marines and the army grew steadily worse.

The Hills of Seoul

Murray's Fifth Marines—already positioned along the north bank of the Han River—initiated the attack on the South Korean capital at 0700. Striking out of the northwest, the U.S. Marines, reinforced by the First Korean Marines, assaulted a series of hills to their front. MacArthur had insisted on using ROK troops for political reasons. He could then say that South Koreans had taken part in the liberation of their capital. The U.S. and ROK Marines faced some ten thousand fresh, well-armed soldiers of the 25th NKPA Brigade, recently arrived from North Korea. The brigade defended a main line of resistance that stretched along a narrow front about three miles long from north to south.

Murray's Third Battalion captured Hill 296 in the north, but failed to drive NK troops off the hill's southern slope where they were strongest. Elements of the Korean Marine Corps assaulted hills 56, 88, and 105-C, which ran west to east in the center sector, but strong enemy fire stopped the KMCs in their tracks. Marine Corsairs struck the hills again and again throughout the day. Despite suffering 40 percent casualties, the North Koreans held. After an all-day battle, Murray's First Battalion seized control of Hill 105-S (one of three hills designated 105).

Little progress was made on September 22, which marked the beginning of a bitter four-day struggle against the hard-nosed, well-emplaced 25th NKPA Brigade. Local real estate would change hands several times daily for the next seventy-two hours.

Twenty-Four Hours or Else

Marine tanks fire upon North Korean attackers while making their way near Seoul in an attempt to soften up the opposition for infantrymen to follow.

With the marines stalled literally at the gates of Seoul on September 23, General Almond reviewed the tactical situation with mounting impatience and displeasure. The chances of sticking to MacArthur's timetable were slipping away, he felt, because the

marines and their tactics were not getting the job done. Almond decided Smith's frontal attack in the west needed an envelopment maneuver from the south. He hurried to Smith's command post to suggest that Smith assign Puller's First Marines to the task.

Smith, fearful of splitting his forces and risking their exposure to friendly fire by approaching the city from separate directions, declined Almond's suggestion. The marine commander preferred to mass his forces and break through the enemy's main line of resistance.

Almond took Smith's refusal to accept the suggested maneuver as equal to disobedience of orders and came close to sacking Smith on the spot. But he feared that the bad politics created by such a dismissal in the field might harm his own military career. Almond instead satisfied his anger by delivering an ultimatum to Smith.

The X Corps commander told Smith to show decisive progress within twenty-four hours or he, Almond, would narrow the marine sector and insert the army's Seventh Infantry Division to get the job done. Then it became Smith's turn to get angry.

Smith later noted in his diary that if Almond thought it necessary to prod marines into action, "he displayed a complete ignorance of the fighting qualities of Marines."

Smith's Ridge

During the night of September 23–24, General Smith began consolidating his division for the first time since it had left the United States. On the morning of September 24, the Fifth Marines continued to press their frontal attack in the west. The First Marines crossed the Han River to form the division's right flank and attack the city from the south. At the same time, Colonel Litzenberg's Seventh Marines crossed the Han to the north of the city. They formed the division's left flank in a move calculated to cut off a North Korean retreat.

The Second Battalion of Murray's Fifth Marines engaged in perhaps the bloodiest fighting of the day on Hill 56. By then the marines had renamed the hill Smith's Ridge, after the company commander of Dog Company, First Lieutenant H. J. Smith. Marines of D and F companies jumped off against the ridgeline in a heavy mist at first light. The F Company marines managed to gain high ground, but heavy NK fire kept D Company pinned down for two hours. Dog Company returned fire and inched forward, finally moving close enough to exchange hand grenades with the NKPA soldiers. Both sides took heavy casualties. The NKs disabled two marine tanks.

When the mist burned off at about 1030, marine Corsairs and artillery pounded away at the hill. Five of ten attacking planes were

U.S. troops advance up the north bank of the Han River in an attempt to break through to Seoul in some of the bloodiest fighting of the war.

badly damaged by NK flak, as the battle became a bloodbath.

By early afternoon, Dog Company was down to forty-four able bodies. Lieutenant Smith decided to gamble and led his survivors in a last desperate charge up the hill. Smith was killed in the charge but his men kept going. Twenty-six marines made it to the crest. Some of the surviving North Koreans fought on briefly, but most of them fled or pretended to be dead. The marines secured the hill.

The battle on Smith's Ridge broke the enemy's defenses north of the Han. North Korean bodies littered the hillside. A marine estimate placed the number of North Korean dead at 1,750. Dog Company casualties numbered 176 out of 206 marines—36 killed, the rest wounded. Marines named the battle "the epic of Dog Company."

A New Low

While the Fifth Marines were slugging it out with the NKPA on Smith's Ridge, General Almond decided not to allow General Smith a full twenty-four hours to show "decisive progress." He was still concerned that the marines were not getting the job done. At 0930 on September 24, Almond notified General Barr and his staff to prepare the Seventh Infantry Division for a thrust at Seoul near Nam-san, or South Mountain.

The X Corps commander then informed marine regimental commanders Puller and Murray at their command posts of the

Direct Control

General Almond insisted on maintaining direct control over all X Corps activities to the point of angering his front-line commanders. But the general felt justified in his actions.

My action was that of a [corps] commander who wants to succeed by coordinating his troops as much as possible. I always announced in advance, in both World War II and Korea, my intention to visit such-and-such units and I usually expected the commanding officer to be present. What I found out, especially in the case of General Smith [the commander of the First Marine Division], was that I could go to the front line and find out for myself the existing conditions more rapidly than I could get them through division headquarters.

Any commander who is concerned about the current situation in any of his major units should go to those units and find out conditions as they exist, as rapidly as possible. If they come through channels, that's fine and if they don't, he can seek them for himself. And by his rapid and frequent visits to the front line fighting units—without disturbing the intermediate commanders concerned—the more

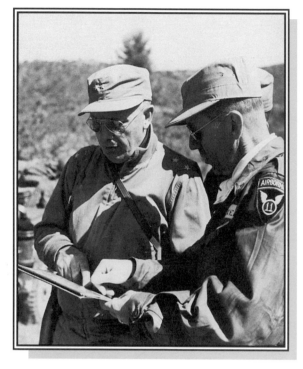

Major General Almond was considered a controversial choice from the start. Many generals thought Almond lacked the experience to head up the Inchon invasion.

his troops learn of the [senior] commander's own feelings about the danger and the objectives.

change in plans. Almond did not bother to advise General Smith. The usually soft-spoken Smith came unglued that afternoon when he learned that Almond had cut him out of the command loop. Smith then "requested" in a demanding tone that Almond quit interfering with his, Smith's, command. Almond did not insist, but his breach of military courtesy had already worsened the existing interservice rivalry.

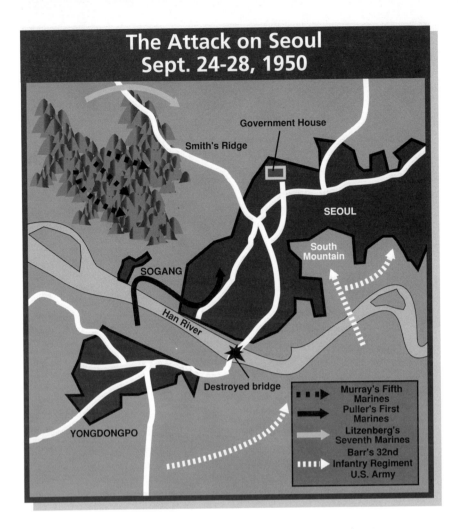

The Attack on Seoul
Sept. 24-28, 1950

Government House

Smith's Ridge

SEOUL

South Mountain

SOGANG

Han River

Destroyed bridge

YONGDONGPO

Murray's Fifth Marines
Puller's First Marines
Litzenberg's Seventh Marines
Barr's 32nd Infantry Regiment U.S. Army

Poor relations between the Marine Corps and the U.S. Army that had taken three years to develop during World War II sank to a new low in Korea in only three months.

Night Action

On the morning of September 25, the Fifth and First Marines moved into the city from the west and south, respectively. At the same time, the 32nd Regiment of the army's Seventh Infantry Division and the 17th ROK Regiment struck the city from the east, mounting an attack on Nam-san. General Almond crossed the Han later that morning to view the action.

That night Almond told a *New York Times* reporter, "The 7th Division is doing a lot of good, very fast." The marines would not get *all* the glory—not if Almond had anything to say about it.

The North Koreans commenced withdrawing their main force, the 18th NKPA Division, late that night. But with the city sealed on all four sides, the North Koreans walked into a trap the next morning. Soldiers from L Company of the 32nd Regiment's Third

The Climax

Major Edwin H. Simmons, who retired from the Marine Corps as a brigadier general, wrote of meeting North Korean troops and tanks along Ma-Po Boulevard on September 24, 1950:

> I was standing in front of this Korean house that I was using as a command post, right by the cellar steps, and a few minutes before two I heard enemy armor clanking down the boulevard toward us.
>
> I flashed a warning over the radio: enemy armor attack. And as I flashed the warning I dove for the cellar steps, kind of all in one motion, as the lead tank fired its first round. I heard the round crack by me, and I looked for my radioman, PFC Vargas, and half of him was on the wall. The first round had gone through his stomach. It was an armor-piercing shell, which was lucky for me, because if it had been high-explosive it very likely would have killed me too.
>
> I called battalion and said, "Let's have artillery. Let's have everything they can shoot."
>
> The artillery fired all night long. And every time they'd stop shooting the tanks would start coming forward again. We're engaging tanks with everything, even machine guns. I could see tracer rounds from the machine guns pinging off the front plates of the enemy tanks. The North Korean infantry got within assaulting distance of us, within burp gun range, but we were solidly dug in and we stopped them rather easily.
>
> This proved to be the climax of the battle for Seoul.

Battalion, led by Lieutenant Harry J. McCaffrey, unexpectedly came upon the retreating North Koreans. McCaffrey ordered an immediate attack. His soldiers waded into battle and killed about five hundred North Koreans and destroyed five tanks. They also destroyed or captured forty vehicles, three artillery pieces, seven machine guns, and a huge supply of ammunition, oil, and clothing. For his part in the action, McCaffrey received the Silver Star.

At about the same time, an eleven-man patrol from the Third Battalion of Puller's First Marines advanced along Ma-Po Boulevard in the center of the city. They were trying to establish contact with Murray's Fifth Marines. Instead, they met a strong enemy force supported by tanks. Patrol leader Corporal Charles E. Collins engaged the NKs in a firefight with his M-1 rifle, while others in his patrol raced back to warn Third Battalion headquarters. Major Edwin H. Simmons called artillery fire down on the NK tanks and infantry, and a fierce battle ensued. By 0630, the Third Battalion marines had destroyed seven tanks, killed 475 North Koreans, and captured 83 more. The Marine Corps rewarded Simmons with the Silver Star.

U.S. Marines engage in street fighting during the liberation of Seoul. Much of the fighting in the city was gritty and bloody as marines went house to house in an attempt to eliminate North Korean opposition.

When asked later by a reporter about the "fleeing enemy," Colonel Chesty Puller said, "All I know about a fleeing enemy is that there's two or three hundred out there that won't be fleeing anywhere."

Speaking to reporters back at X Corps headquarters, General Almond said, "Nothing could have been more fortunate than the tank-led enemy counterattacks. It gave us a greater opportunity to kill more enemy soldiers and to destroy his tanks more easily than if we had to take the city house by house."

The results of the night's action prompted MacArthur to release United Nations Communiqué 9, which stated in part:

Seoul, the capital of the Republic of South Korea, is again in friendly hands. United Nations Forces, including the 17th Regiment of the ROK Army and elements of the U.S. 7th Infantry and 1st Marine Divisions, have completed the envelopment of the city.

But much fighting still lay ahead and many would die the next day. Most of the dirty, deadly work—the house-to-house clearing away of a dug-in, fanatical enemy—was accomplished by the men of the First Marine Division.

The Final Days

The liberation of Seoul was not a pretty sight. Most of the South Korean capital was destroyed in the process. British correspondent Reginald Thompson of the London *Daily Telegraph* described it this way:

> It is an appalling inferno of din and destruction with the tearing noise of dive bombers blasting right ahead, and the livid flashes of the tank guns, the harsh, fierce crackle of blazing wooden buildings, telegraph and high-tension poles collapsing in utter chaos of wires. Great palls of smoke lie over us as massive buildings collapse in showers of sparks, puffing masses of smoke and rubble upon us in terrific heat. . . . Few people can have suffered so terrible a liberation.

North Korean prisoners are herded down a village street by a U.S. tank.

(Above) A U.S. soldier raises the Stars and Stripes above the American consulate in Seoul upon the liberation of the city. (Right) General Douglas MacArthur at the ceremony to restore the Republic of Korea to President Syngman Rhee.

The end finally came when the Fifth Marines seized Chang-dok Palace and Government House on the afternoon of September 27, yanking down North Korean flags and raising the Stars and Stripes.

On September 29, 1950, General of the Army Douglas MacArthur returned the city to South Korean president Syngman Rhee in a noontime address at the National Assembly Hall in Seoul: "In behalf of the United Nations Command I am happy to restore to you, Mr. President, the seat of your government, that from it you may better fulfill your constitutional responsibilities."

The next day, President Harry S. Truman sent a message to MacArthur, part of which said:

> No operations in military history can match either the delaying action where you traded space for time in which to build up your forces, or the brilliant maneuver which has now resulted in the liberation of Seoul. . . . I salute you all, and say to all, from all of us at home, "Well and nobly done."

AFTERWORD

A Change for the Worse

The First Marine Division and Seventh Infantry Division, supported by ROK Army and Marine Corps units, completely cleared Seoul of enemy troops on September 28, 1950. Elements of the First Marine Division pressed on toward Munsan and Uijongbu until relieved by EUSA units on October 7, 1950. Operation CHROMITE ended.

Marines prepare to raise the Stars and Stripes above Seoul after its successful liberation.

Three More Years

The decision that prolonged the Korean agony for nearly three more years came to MacArthur in a message from the Joint Chiefs of Staff on September 27, 1950. The message said:

> Your military objective is the destruction of the North Korean armed forces. In attaining this objective, you are authorized to conduct military operations, including amphibious and airborne landings or ground operations north of the 38th Parallel in Korea, provided that at the time of such operations there has been no entry into North Korea by major Soviet or Chinese Communist Forces, no announcement of intended entry, nor a threat to counter our operations militarily in North Korea.

> Under no circumstances, however, will your forces cross the Manchurian or U.S.S.R. borders of Korea and, as a matter of policy, no non-Korean ground forces will be used in the northeast provinces bordering the Soviet Union or in the area along the Manchurian border. Furthermore, support of your operations north or south of the 38th Parallel will not include air or naval action against Manchuria or against U.S.S.R. territory.

A war that might have ended at the 38th parallel would now last until July 27, 1953. And more than fifty-four thousand Americans would die in the rice paddies, hills, and mountains of Korea.

During the twenty-three-day operation, X Corps killed some 14,000 NKPA troops and captured about 7,000 more. The First Marine Division suffered 2,450 battle casualties. Their losses included 366 killed in action, 2,029 wounded in action, and 6 missing in action. Forty-nine later died of wounds. Casualties of the Seventh Infantry Division totaled 572, with 106 killed in action, 409 wounded in action, and 57 missing in action.

General MacArthur gambled at Inchon and won a great victory, thereby restoring South Korea to the South Koreans. The invasion achieved total operational and tactical success. Some military analysts believe that Operation CHROMITE was *too* successful in that it led to a change in political goals.

Encouraged by the "easy" victory at Inchon, the United States and the United Nations decided to cross the 38th parallel, destroy what was left of the NKPA , and unify Korea under a single, popularly elected government. This decision extended the Korean War for nearly three more long and bloody years.

The worst was yet to come.

Glossary

battalion: A body of troops made up of headquarters and two or more companies or batteries.

battery: A grouping of artillery pieces for tactical purposes.

brigade: A military unit smaller than a division and larger than a regiment, with attached groups and/or battalions as needed to meet anticipated requirements.

buffer state: A neutral state lying between two larger and potentially hostile states.

bunker: A fortified structure for the protection of personnel and armament (such as machine guns) in a defensive position.

causeway: A raised thoroughfare across wet ground or water.

CINCFE: Commander in Chief, Far East.

division: A tactical combat unit or formation larger than a regiment or brigade but smaller than a corps.

-do: Korean word for "island."

dominion: Supreme authority.

envelopment: A two-part attack consisting of a frontal attack to hold the enemy and a flanking attack to envelop him.

EUSA: Eighth United States Army.

firefight: A brief, intense exchange of fire between infantry units.

foxhole: A small hole used for cover and to fight out of by one or two people.

friendly fire: Small-arms fire, artillery, rockets, bombs, etc., mistakenly directed against one's own side, especially in battle.

GI: Literally, government issue; an American enlisted person.

I Corps: Eye Corps; a component of the Eighth U.S. Army; principally the 24th Infantry and First Cavalry Divisions.

insubordinate: Disobedient to authority.

JCS: Joint Chiefs of Staff.

KMAG: Korea Military Advisory Group.

Medal of Honor: Highest U.S. award for bravery in combat.

mopping up: The elimination of remnants of enemy resistance in an area through which other units have passed without destroying all enemy opposition.

napalm: A powder used to thicken gasoline for use in flamethrowers and incendiary bombs.

Navy Cross: Second-highest U.S. Navy and Marine Corps award for bravery in combat.

-ni: Korean word for "ridge."

IX Corps: Ninth Corps; a component of the Eighth U.S. Army; principally the Second and 25th Infantry Divisions.

NK: North Korean.

NKPA: North Korean People's Army.

Operation CHROMITE: Code name assigned to the Inchon invasion.

phosphorus: A self-igniting (in the air) chemical element that gives off a dense white smoke; used in grenades and artillery shells to form a protective smoke screen.

platoon: A subdivision of a tactical unit such as a company, usually commanded by a lieutenant.

R&R: Rest and recuperation.

regiment: A military unit larger than a battalion and smaller than a division.

regimental combat team (RCT): A task organization of troops for amphibious operations.

ROK: Republic of (South) Korea.

ROKA: Republic of Korea Army.

-san: Korean word for "mountain."

SCAP: Supreme Commander, Allied Powers.

seawall: A wall that protects the shore from erosion or acts as a breakwater.

section: A tactical unit of the U.S. Army or Marine Corps smaller than a platoon and larger than a squad.

Silver Star: Third-highest U.S. award for bravery in combat.

sovereign: Independent (as an independent state).

squad: A small party of soldiers grouped for tactical or other purposes.

strategy: The planning and directing of the entire operation of a war or campaign (*see also* tactics).

suzerain: A dominant state that controls the foreign relations of another state and exacts payment from the lesser state.

tactics: The art of placing or maneuvering forces skillfully in a battle (see also strategy).

Tan'gun: Founder of Korea (in 2333 B.C.).

Task Force Kean: Task force combining the First Provisional Marine Brigade, the 35th Infantry Regiment and the Fifth Regimental Combat Team; used to launch the first American counterattack of the Korean War.

Task Force Lynch: Task force formed by the reinforced Third Battalion of the Seventh Cavalry Regiment; used to spearhead Eighth Army's northward drive to link up with X Corps.

Task Force Smith: Task force made up of 440 men from First Battalion, 21st Infantry Regiment, 24th Infantry Division; named for its commander, Lieutenant Colonel Charles B. "Brad" Smith; the first U.S. unit to fight in the Korean War.

X Corps: Tenth Corps; Inchon invasion force comprising the First Marine and Seventh Infantry Divisions and various support groups.

trench: A ditch to protect soldiers from gunfire.

ultimatum: A final proposition, condition, or demand.

vanguard: An element of the advanced guard.

For Further Reading

James Brady, *The Coldest War: A Memoir of Korea.* New York: Orion Books, 1990. A popular columnist tells the story of his life as a young marine lieutenant during the Korean War. Sensitive and beautifully written.

Charles M. Bussey, *Firefight at Yechon: Courage and Racism in the Korean War.* New York: Macmillan, 1991. A disturbing account of heroism and racism in the U.S. Army during the Korean War, written by a decorated, retired lieutenant colonel whose army combat experiences affirm that racists exist even in foxholes.

D. M. Giangreco, *War in Korea 1950–1953.* Novato, CA: Presidio Press, 1990. A pictorial history of the Korean War that "presents the conflict with incredible clarity." Contains over five hundred vivid photographs that dramatically portray "frozen instants in a war that is now largely forgotten."

Arned L. Hinshaw, *Heartbreak Ridge: Korea, 1951.* New York: Praeger Publishers, 1989. A doctor-lawyer whose active and reserve military career spans forty-one years writes a compelling story of the famous battle that was expected to be over in a day but continued for a full month of bloody sacrifice.

William B. Hopkins, *One Bugle, No Drums: The Marines at Chosin Reservoir.* New York: Avon Books, 1986. A riveting account of marines under desperate fire at the Chosin Reservoir, written by the company commander of a marine headquarters and service company in Korea.

D. Clayton James, with Anne Sharp Wells, *Refighting the Last War: Command and Crisis in Korea 1950–1953.* New York: Free Press, 1993. Written by one of America's foremost historians, this scholarly work examines the roles of five high-ranking American commanders in the Korean War and looks at the six crucial issues confronting them in that conflict.

Donald Knox, with additional text by Alfred Coppel, *The Korean War: Uncertain Victory.* San Diego: Harvest/HBJ Book, Harcourt Brace Jovanovich, 1988. An oral history of the last two and one-half years of the Korean War, told through the reflections and remembrances of those who fought to win an "uneasy armistice" and an "uncertain victory." Puts the reader there.

S. L. A. Marshall, *Pork Chop Hill: The American Fighting Man in Action, Korea, Spring 1953.* Nashville, TN: Battery Press, (Book Club edition; no date given). The story of the Seventh Infantry Division's forty-eight-hour defense of a tiny Korean hill against human waves of determined Chinese attackers. A deeply moving work by the late dean of American military historians.

————, *The River and the Gauntlet: The Battle of the Chongchon River, Korea 1950.* Nashville, TN: Battery Press (Book Club Edition; no date given). The eminent historian describes the gallant efforts of two U.S. infantry divisions to delay successive waves of Chinese attackers in the rugged mountains of north-central Korea.

Jim Wilson, *Retreat, Hell! We're Just Attacking in Another Direction.* New York: William Morrow, 1988. The epic story of the First Marine Division's fighting withdrawal from the Chosin Reservoir to Hungnam, told by a veteran reporter who served with the U.S. Army in Korea during that war.

Works Consulted

Bevin Alexander, *Korea: The First War We Lost.* New York: Hippocrene Books, 1986. The story of how America *won* one war by stopping North Korean aggression and *lost* another by trying to destroy the North Korean state.

Clay Blair, *The Forgotten War: America in Korea 1950–1953.* New York: Times Books, 1987. A definitive account of America's "forgotten war" in Korea, written by a top-ranking American military historian. Emphasizes the role of the U.S. Army and the combat infantryman during the Korean War.

————, *MacArthur.* Garden City, NY: Nelson Doubleday, 1977. A highly readable biography of one of America's greatest war heroes and most controversial military leaders. Includes excellent coverage of the Inchon invasion.

Omar N. Bradley and Clay Blair, *A General's Life.* New York: Simon & Schuster, 1983. A fine account of the life of one of America's greatest generals, written by the general with one of the country's greatest military historians.

David Douglas Duncan, *This Is War! A Photo-Narrative of the Korean War.* Boston: Little Brown, 1990. A masterwork of photographic narrative by a former combat marine and world-renowned, prize-winning photographer. This is truly war!

R. Ernest Dupuy and Trevor N. Dupuy, *The Encyclopedia of Military History.* New York: Harper & Row, 1977. A monumental work on warfare by two noted historians. Includes a keen analysis of the Inchon invasion.

Trevor N. Dupuy, Curt John, and David L. Bongard, *The Harper Encyclopedia of Military Biography.* New York: HarperCollins, 1992. The researcher's sourcebook for information about the lives of major figures in military history.

Robert J. Dvorchak and the writers and photographers of the Associated Press, *Battle for Korea: The Associated Press History of the Korean Conflict.* Conshohocken, PA: Combined Books, 1993. The writers and photographers of the Associated Press who witnessed the battle for Korea firsthand present its story in lucid prose and telling photographs. Captures the essence of combat in a far-off place.

Joseph C. Goulden, *Korea: The Untold Story of the War.* New York: Times Books, 1982. A revealing narrative covering every aspect of the Korean War, including its spectacular military actions, its political origins, its tormented peace process, and subsequent consequences.

Max Hastings, *The Korean War.* New York: Touchstone Books, Simon & Schuster, 1987. Using personal accounts from interviews with more than two hundred veterans—including the Chinese—one of the ablest of the younger generation of British military historians grips readers with a splendid history of the "first war we could not win."

Edwin P. Hoyt, *On to the Yalu.* Briarcliff Manor, NY: Stein and Day, 1984. The author of many naval and military histories describes three crucial months of the Korean War, from MacArthur's military success at Inchon to the Chinese intervention in November 1950.

William Manchester, *American Caesar: Douglas MacArthur: 1880–1964.* Boston: Little, Brown, 1978. A definitive biography of "a great thundering paradox of a man" that "challenges the cherished myths of MacArthur's fans and critics alike." The author, a noted biographer, served in combat with the U.S. Marines in the South Pacific during World War II.

Lynn Montross and Captain Nicholas A. Canzona, *U.S. Marine Operations in Korea 1950–1953*, vol. 1: *The Pusan Perimeter*. Washington, DC: Government Printing Office, 1954. The official U.S. Marine Corps account of the fighting in the Pusan perimeter.

J. Robert Moskin, *The Story of the United States Marine Corps*. New York & London: The Paddington Press, 1979. A history of the Marine Corps from 1775 through 1975. Includes excellent coverage of the marines' role in Korea.

John Quick, *Dictionary of Weapons & Military Terms*. New York: McGraw-Hill, 1973. A comprehensive record of the significant weapons developed over the centuries by armies all over the world.

Shelby L. Stanton, *America's Tenth Legion: X Corps in Korea, 1950*. Novato, CA: Presidio Press, 1989. A prominent military historian tells the story of the critical X Corps campaign on both coasts of Korea, from its landing at Inchon through its drive to the Yalu River and final evacuation at Hungnam.

Harry G. Summers Jr., *Korean War Almanac*. New York: Facts on File, 1990. A well-researched and objective presentation of every aspect of the Korean War, written by a retired infantry colonel who is a decorated veteran of the Korean and Vietnam Wars.

John Toland, *In Mortal Combat: Korea, 1950–1953*. New York: William Morrow, 1991. A brilliant narrative of the Korean War, from its unexpected start through its unresolved finish. Stresses personal interviews.

Rudy Tomedi, *No Bugles, No Drums: An Oral History of the Korean War*. New York: John Wiley & Sons, 1993. A journalist shares the deeply personal experiences and remembrances of the warriors who fought in the killing ground called Korea.

Appendix: Aircraft, Arms, and Armor Used in the Inchon Invasion

Amtrac: A nine-ton, amphibious personnel landing vehicle used by the U.S. Army and Marine Corps. It could operate at speeds of 6 mph on water and 30 mph on land with a range of 190 miles. It was manufactured by Borg-Warner (*see also* LVT).

Browning water-cooled machine gun: The .30-caliber machine gun M1917A1. A tripod-mounted, recoil-operated, water-cooled machine gun, 38.5 inches long, weighing 41 pounds with water. The mount weighs 53.15 pounds. The gun fires at a rate of 450–600 rounds a minute, using a 250-round fabric belt or disintegrating link belt. It was the standard battalion-level, rifle-caliber machine gun used by the United States during World War II and the Korean War.

burp gun: The Soviet Pistolet-Pulemyot Shpagina obr 1941G (PPSh41) submachine gun or its Chinese-made counterpart; the most famous small arm of the Korean War. It fired a 7.62mm bullet at a rate of 900 rounds a minute, using either a 35- or 75-round magazine. Its name derived from the distinctive sound of its rapid fire. A cheap, crudely made, but effective weapon.

C-54 Skymaster: The Douglas Skymaster was a four-engine military transport developed from the DC-4. First flown in 1939, it was widely used in World War II and was still in use during the Korean War. It could carry about 30,000 pounds at speeds up to 250 mph over a normal range of 1,500 miles.

Corsair: The Vought F4U Corsair was a single-seat, single-engine shipboard fighter and fighter-bomber. The Corsair was developed for the U.S. Navy and first flown in May 1940. It was used extensively against the Japanese in the Pacific during World War II, and later as a fighter-bomber in the Korean War. The first U.S. fighter to exceed 400 mph, the Corsair reached speeds of 446 mph and was armed with six .50-caliber machine guns. It carried two 1,000-pound bombs or eight 5-inch rockets.

Browning water-cooled machine gun

burp gun

Vought F4U Corsair

F-51 Mustang: The North American P- or F-51 Mustang was a single-seat, single-engine, long-range fighter and fighter-bomber. First flown in October 1940, it soon established itself as one of the finest fighters of World War II. It was also used in Korea, primarily as a fighter-bomber. It flew at speeds of 437 mph and was armed with six .50-caliber machine guns. It could carry two 500-pound bombs or one 1,000-pound bomb or six 5-inch rockets.

five-inch gun: U.S. 5-inch/54 naval gun. This U.S. shipboard weapon fires a 70-pound projectile at a firing rate of 15-18 rounds a minute. It has a horizontal range of about 26,000 yards and an effective ceiling of approximately 49,000 feet.

grenade: A small explosive or chemical missile of varied design. Grenades may be classified as hand or rifle grenades. More recently grenades are designed to be projected from special grenade launchers.

LC: Any of a wide variety of landing craft.

LCVP: A U.S. Navy vehicle and personnel landing craft; a small amphibious assault boat capable of beaching.

LSMR: A U.S. Navy medium landing ship (rocket).

LST: Landing ship, tank. U.S. LST 1–1152 classes of World War II and Korean War vintage carried 211 troops and a cargo of 2,100 tons at a speed of 11 knots. They measured 316 feet in length, weighed 1,653 tons, and were armed with two 20mm and seven 40mm antiaircraft guns. Troops often called them "Large Slow Targets."

LVT: A U.S. Navy landing vehicle, tracked (see also Amtrac).

M-1 rifle: The .30-caliber M-1 rifle (Garand semiautomatic rifle) is a gas-operated, semiautomatic rifle, 43.6 inches long, weighing 9.5 pounds, with an effective range of 500 yards. It uses an eight-round ammunition clip. It was the basic U.S. infantry weapon during World War II and the Korean War.

F-51 Mustang

U.S. fragmentation grenade used in World War II and Korea. Also known as "pineapple" grenade.

LC (landing craft)

LST

M-26 tank: The "General Pershing"; a medium tank mounting a 90mm gun; used by U.S. forces in Korea at the start of the war.

M4A3 tank: U.S. tank, medium, M4A3. The "General Sherman" tank carried a crew of five and was armed with one M3 75mm gun and two M1919A4 .30-caliber machine guns. It weighed 36 tons and reached speeds of 25 mph on roads.

MiG-17: The Mikoyan/Gurevich MiG-17 single-seat jet fighter and fighter-bomber was developed for use in the Soviet Air Force but used by at least fifteen other countries, including North Korea and China. It flew at a speed of about Mach .975 (721.5 mph) at a range of 750 miles and was armed with three 23mm cannons, plus four 8-rocket pods or two 550-pound bombs.

mortars: High-angle-fire weapons, particularly suited for use in Korea's mountainous terrain. U.S. forces used 60mm (light), 81mm (medium), and 4.2-inch (heavy) mortars. North Korean and Chinese forces used 61mm, 82mm, and 120mm mortars. The 61mm and 82mm mortar bores, which were slightly larger than their U.S. equivalents, could fire captured U.S. ammunition.

PM water-cooled machine gun: The most commonly used water-cooled machine gun used by North Korean and Chinese forces was the Soviet recoil-operated, belt-fed, 7.62mm PM (Pulemyot Maxima) 1910 model. Usually mounted on a "Sokolov" wheeled carriage, the 7.62mm PM fired at a rate of about 600 rounds a minute.

Sabre jet: The North American F-86 Sabre was a single-seat, single-engine jet tactical fighter and fighter-bomber developed for the U.S. Air Force and first flown in 1947. It became the first swept-wing U.S. jet to see combat (in Korea). The F-86F had a speed of 687 mph and a range of 1000 miles. Armed with six .50-caliber machine guns, it could carry two Sidewinder missiles or two 1,000-pound bombs. In air battles with MiG-17s over

M-26 tank

M4A3 tanks

F-86 Sabre jets

Korea, American pilots flying Sabre jets racked up a kill ratio of 14:1.

75mm recoilless rifle: A 75mm weapon consisting of a light-artillery tube and a lightweight, portable tripod mount. It can also be mounted in light vehicles such as jeeps. Recoil is eliminated by the controlled release of propellant gases to the rear through a breechblock opening.

T-34 tank: The Soviet-built T-34 medium tank mounted a high-velocity 85mm main gun and possessed exceptional cross-country mobility. The North Korean People's Army was equipped with 120 such tanks at the start of the Korean War. The T-34 was considered to be one of the finest medium tanks produced during World War II.

3.5-inch rocket launcher: The later model 3.5-inch rocket launcher named the "super-bazooka" was a larger version of the original bazooka. It fired an 8.5-pound rocket that possessed double the armor-piercing power of the 3.5-pound missile, making it highly effective for use against tanks.

2.36-inch rocket launcher: Popularly called the "bazooka" (after an odd musical instrument used by American comedian Bob Burns), the 2.36-inch rocket launcher fired a 3.5-pound missile with a range of up to 400 yards. This breech-loading weapon weighed about 12 pounds and measured 54 inches long.

V-T fuze: A variable-time fuze designed to detonate artillery shells, bombs, mines, or other charges by external influence other than contact in the target area.

75mm recoilless rifle

Soviet T-34 tank

3.5-inch rocket launcher (bazooka)

Index

Picture Credits

Cover photo: National Archives

AP/Wide World Photos, 103 (bottom)

The Bettman Archive, 13

Library of Congress, 15 (left), 25

National Archives, 14, 16, 21, 27 (both), 30 (right), 31, 32, 34, 38, 40, 42 (both), 43, 44 (both), 45, 47, 49, 51, 52, 53, 54, 55, 58, 61 (both), 62, 64 (both), 66 (both), 68, 70, 72, 73, 76, 77, 79 (both), 81, 85, 86, 88, 89, 92, 93, 94 (both), 95, 102 (bottom), 103 (middle), 104 (bottom), 105 (top)

Stock Montage, Inc., 11, 12

UPI/Bettmann, 15 (right), 83, 103 (top), 104 (top and middle), 105 (middle and bottom)

The Washington Post by permission of the D.C. Library, 18, 19, 22, 23, 30 (left), 36, 60

West Point Museum, 102 (top and middle)

About the Author

Earle Rice Jr. attended San Jose City College and Foothill College on the San Francisco peninsula, after serving nine years with the U.S. Marine Corps. Mr. Rice served in Korea with the First Marine Division during that war, as a machine-gun squad leader in George Company, Third Battalion, First Marines.

He has authored ten books for young adults, including adaptations of *Dracula* and *All Quiet on the Western Front*. Mr. Rice most recently wrote *The Battle of Midway* for Lucent Books. He has also written articles and short stories, and he worked for several years as a technical writer.

Mr. Rice is a retired senior design engineer from the aerospace industry who devotes full time to writing. He lives in Julian, California, with his wife, daughter, granddaughter, two cats, and a dog.